BASEBALL'S
GREATEST
GAMES

• • • • • • • • • • • • • •

Dan Gutman

VIKING

VIKING
Published by the Penguin Group
Penguin Books USA Inc., 375 Hudson Street, New York, New York 10014, U.S.A.
Penguin Books Ltd, 27 Wrights Lane, London W8 5TZ, England
Penguin Books Australia Ltd, Ringwood, Victoria, Australia
Penguin Books Canada Ltd, 10 Alcorn Avenue, Toronto, Ontario, Canada M4V 3B2
Penguin Books (N.Z.) Ltd, 182–190 Wairau Road, Auckland 10, New Zealand

Penguin Books Ltd, Registered Offices: Harmondsworth, Middlesex, England

First published in 1994 by Viking, a division of Penguin Books USA Inc.

1   3   5   7   9   10   8   6   4   2

Library of Congress Cataloging-in-Publication Data
Gutman, Dan.
Baseball's greatest games / by Dan Gutman.   p.   cm.
ISBN 0-670-84604-X
1. Baseball—United States—History.   I. Title.   GV863.A1G865   1994
796.357'0973—dc20   93-31504   CIP

Printed in U.S.A.   Set in 11 pt. Aster

To Nina,
who always comes through
when I'm down a run in the bottom of the ninth

Acknowledgments

The following baseball experts were kind enough to offer their
recommendations of baseball's greatest games: Paul Adomites,
Charles Alexander, Bob Buege, Bob Carroll, Bill Deane, Morris Eckhouse,
Chuck Hershberger, John Holway, Ralph Horton, W. Lloyd Johnson,
Roger Kahn, Jack Lang, Scott McKinstry, Daniel Okrent,
David Pietrusza, George Robinson, and David Quentin Voigt.

Also, I want to express my thanks to Michele Chism, Leigh Connor,
Carol Ellerman, Pat Kelly, Michael Lattman, Elizabeth Law, David Plaut,
JoAnn Pure, Doug Rauschenberger, Cecilia Yung, and the public libraries of
St. Louis, Philadelphia, Chicago, Brooklyn, and Haddonfield, New Jersey.

NOTE TO READERS:

Even the greatest games ever played had innings in which nothing significant happened. Rather than bore you with details of those innings in this book, they have been left out of the play-by-play. So if the description of a game jumps from the fifth inning to the seventh inning, that means the sixth inning was uneventful and had no bearing on the final score.

Contents

Introduction   ix

The Stars of This Book   1

1. *The Shot Heard 'Round the World*   2
Probably the greatest baseball game ever played.

2. *The Fisk Game*   26
Game 6, 1975. They're still talking about this one
in Boston.

3. *The Haddix Game*   48
The best game ever pitched in major league history.
Sometimes being perfect isn't good enough.

4. *The Mazeroski Game*   68
A slugfest between the mighty Yankees and the lowly
Pirates to conclude the 1960 World Series.

5. *The $15,000 "Slide"*   92
The most famous game of the 19th century.

6. *The Houston Marathon*   114
Sixteen suspenseful innings that decided the 1986
National League pennant.

7. *The Homer in the Gloamin'*   136
The 1938 pennant on the line. Darkness descended
on the field, and there were no lights to turn on.

8. *The Alexander Game*   158
A classic confrontation between the over-the-hill
veteran and the rookie phenom in the tense 7th game
of the 1926 World Series.

9. *The Gibson Game*   184
One for the ages. The first game in the 1988 World Series.

Want to Read More About These Stories?   204

Index   206

Introduction

WHO'S TO SAY what were the greatest games in baseball history?

Certainly not *me*. I didn't see most of the games described in this book. I wasn't even *born* when half of them were played.

That's why I contacted baseball historians around the country to ask what *they* thought were the greatest games ever played. Roger Kahn *(The Boys of Summer)* suggested Game 5 of the 1952 World Series. Charles Alexander *(Ty Cobb)* mentioned the Vaughn/Toney double no-hitter in 1917. David Quentin Voigt *(American Baseball)* told me to "pick out a slug fest—like the Phils/Cubs game in the 1980s when both teams scored in the 20s!" Dan Okrent *(The Ultimate Baseball Book)* said the greatest game he ever saw was a Double A game between the Pittsfield Cubs and New Britain Red Sox in 1986. The results of that survey are the games you'll read about on the following pages.

This book was written by poring over accounts of the games in newspapers, books, magazines, radio broadcasts, and sometimes videos. I combined them all to create a play-by-play, often pitch-by-pitch replay of the action. If I succeeded, you should be able to imagine that you're sitting in the bleachers watching the greatest ball games ever played.

Everything here, to the best of my knowledge, is true. If it says a guy doubled to left center-field, the ball *didn't* go down the first baseline. If it says a guy tugged at his cap or shouted "Let 'er rip!" he *did*. No quotes were made up. Nothing was invented for the sake of drama. These games were dramatic enough without the need to juice them up with phony excitement.

WHAT MAKES A GREAT GAME? Dominating pitching? Long home runs? Spectacular catches in the field? Brilliant strategy?

Yes. Yes. Yes. Yes. But most of all, a great game is a game with *tension*. It could be a scoreless pitcher's duel going into the bottom of the 13th inning. Or it could be a 12–11 slugfest. When the lead changes hands a few times, that almost always makes for a thrilling ball game.

The games in this book, with the exception of the one in Chapter 3, all took place at the end of the season, when tension hangs over the diamond even before the first pitch is thrown.

There have certainly been plenty of great games in the beginning or middle of baseball season, and they count as much as games at the end. But they're almost always forgotten because 50, 75 or even 100 or more games remain before the final standings are decided.

In the long run, a great game is a game that people remember years, even decades, after it took place. Its story is passed down through generations of baseball fans. It is not an exaggeration to say that the games described in this book will be remembered as long as baseball exists. *Centuries.*

My only regret is that there are so many great games that couldn't fit between these covers. Johnny Vander Meer's second consecutive no-hitter in 1938. Game 7 of the 1977 World Series, when Reggie Jackson slammed three home runs on three pitches. Don Larsen's perfect game in 1956. Babe Ruth's "called shot" in 1932.

There are so many others. I wish I had been able to include them all.

—Dan Gutman

The Stars of This Book
(In Order of Appearance)

Willie Mays

Leo Durocher

Duke Snider

Jackie Robinson

Bobby Thomson

Ralph Branca

Pete Rose

Joe Morgan

Johnny Bench

Luis Tiant

Carl Yastrzemski

Carlton Fisk

Henry Aaron

Eddie Mathews

Roberto Clemente

Harvey Haddix

Mickey Mantle

Roger Maris

Casey Stengel

Yogi Berra

Bill Mazeroski

Adrian "Cap" Anson

Mike "King" Kelly

Arlie Latham

Curt Welch

Mike Scott

Bob Ojeda

Gary Carter

Lenny Dykstra

Keith Hernandez

Darryl Strawberry

Ray Knight

Jesse Orosco

Grover Cleveland Alexander

Babe Ruth

Lou Gehrig

Rogers Hornsby

Gabby Hartnett

Kirk Gibson

Jose Canseco

Dennis Eckersley

CHAPTER
1

The Shot
Heard 'Round the World

THE DATE: Wednesday, October 3, 1951.
THE PLACE: The Polo Grounds, New York City.
THE SITUATION: Third and final game
of the playoff series between the New York Giants
and Brooklyn Dodgers. The game would decide
the National League pennant.

Bobby Thomson (George Brace)

Ralph Branca. He was so good, he had tryouts with three major league teams by the time he was 17. (NBL)

long will be remembered as the most thrilling pennant campaign in history, Leo Durocher and his astounding never-say-die Giants

*Y*OUR GRANDPARENTS PROBABLY remember exactly where they were and what they were doing when news of the Pearl Harbor invasion hit the airwaves. Your parents probably remember exactly where they were when John F. Kennedy and Martin Luther King, Jr., were shot, and when Neil Armstrong set foot on the moon. Younger people remember the moment they heard that the space shuttle Challenger had exploded.

And almost everyone old enough to remember 1951 remembers exactly what they were doing at 3:58 on October 3 of that year. In most cases, they were screaming their heads off, either with joy or frustration. It was the moment of "the Shot Heard 'Round the World"—the dramatic ending to the most gripping pennant race ever and very possibly the most exciting moment in baseball history.

IT DIDN'T LOOK LIKE it was going to be much of a race when baseball season began. The New York Giants won their opening game, then dropped the next 11 in a row. The Brooklyn Dodgers, who had won the National League flag in 1947 and 1949, jumped right into first place by winning 28 of their first 36 games. They were a powerhouse, and would lead the league in runs, doubles, home runs, batting average, slugging average, stolen bases, and double plays.

The Giants were desperate for some kind of spark plug to ignite the team, so in May they brought up a 20-year-old kid from Alabama who was hitting .477 and chasing down fly balls like a gazelle for their Minneapolis Millers farm team. You know the kid's name—Willie Mays. Mays's father, also named Willie, had played for the Birmingham Black Barons of the Negro League.

Right away, Willie came to be called The Say Hey Kid because he had trouble remembering names and would say "Say Hey!" when he greeted people.

He also had trouble hitting in the big leagues. The young phenom went 0 for 12 in his first three games, including six strikeouts. After that third game, Giants manager Leo "the Lip" Durocher found Willie sitting in front of his locker, with his head in his hands, tears running down his face. Durocher came over to see what was the matter, and Mays sobbed, "I know I can't play up here, and you're gonna send me back to Minneapolis. That's where I belong. I don't belong up here."

Durocher told Willie he was the Giants center fielder no matter what, and the next day Mays launched his first major league hit, a towering homer off Hall of Famer Warren Spahn that sailed over the left field wall of the Polo Grounds.

But after that Willie went *another* 13 at-bats without a hit, and his big league career started at 1 hit in 26 plate appearances. That's a batting average of .038.

A FEW MORE NUMBERS for you statistics lovers: On June 1, the Dodgers had a 24–15 record and a 4½ game lead on the rest of the National League. The Giants were in fifth place, at 21–21. At the All-Star break, the Giants were in second place, but 8½ games back. On August 5, they were 9½ games back. On August 11, they were 13 games back. At that point, there were just 44 games left in the season.

It was a hopeless situation. *Nobody* makes up that much ground.

WHEN THEY WERE AT THEIR LOWEST, something happened that turned the season around for the Giants. At the Polo Grounds, where the Giants played their home games, there was a thin wooden wall that separated the home team and visiting team clubhouses. After the Dodgers swept a three-game series to send the Giants 12 games back, the Brooklyn boys couldn't resist rubbing it in. As a team, they pounded on the wall, shouting, "The Giants are dead! The Giants are dead! How do you like it now, Leo?"

The Giants decided they'd suffered enough humiliation at the hands of the Dodgers. They vowed they would get revenge.

Quite suddenly, everything turned around. Willie Mays found the groove that would eventually make him one of the greatest players to ever step on a baseball diamond. Giants third baseman Bobby Thomson, a .270 lifetime hitter, started tearing up the league at nearly a .400 clip. The Giants began to win consistently. At one point they peeled off 16 victories in a row.

Meanwhile, the Dodgers were floundering. The pitchers ran out of gas. The hitters stopped hitting. They didn't totally collapse, but they were losing as often as they were winning.

With 26 games left in the season, the Giants had climbed within five games of the Dodgers, and the newspapers began to refer to them as "The Creeping Terror." Nothing could stop them. The Giants won 37 of their last 44 games. (That's an unbelievable .841 winning percentage.) After losing 10 of their first 11 games to *start* the season, they won 10 of their last 11 to *finish* it.

When the dust had cleared, the Giants and Dodgers ended the 1951 season in a dead heat. After 154 games (today they play 162), both teams had records of 96 wins and 58 losses. A three-game playoff would decide the National League pennant.

THE 1951 NATIONAL LEAGUE playoff was one of the first sporting events to be televised coast-to-coast. Many American families hadn't bought their first TV set in 1951, and now they had a reason to get one. General Electric had a playoff special on their Black Daylite model—$80 off.

The three playoff games blared from radios in every barber shop, store, and apartment. Strangers walked up to one another on the street to ask, "What's the score?"

The rivalry between the Dodgers and the Giants was probably the oldest and most bitter in sports. They were the only two major league teams in history to compete in the same city in the same league. The nation, and especially New York City, was captivated.

THE GIANTS WON the first game 3–1 when Bobby Thomson hit a two-run homer off Dodgers pitcher Ralph Branca. It was Thomson's second home run of the season off Branca.

In Game 2, Brooklyn evened things out when Clem Labine shut out the Giants while Dodgers hitters pounded out ten runs.

The pennant would be decided by one final, climactic game. This is the game that is most often mentioned as the greatest game in baseball history.

IT WAS A WEDNESDAY, and the newspapers say skies were overcast that day. That didn't stop celebrities like Frank Sinatra, Jackie Gleason, Tallulah Bankhead, and FBI chief J. Edgar Hoover from coming out to the Polo Grounds. Four high-school students had camped out all night waiting for the ticket office to open. It's safe to say that many of the kids who stayed home from school that Wednesday weren't all that sick.

Most of the members of the New York Yankees were at the ballpark, too. They had already clinched the American League pennant and were anxious to see who they would be facing in the World Series.

Naturally, the Dodgers and Giants each sent their best pitcher to the mound. For the Giants, that was 34-year-old Sal "the Barber" Maglie, a junkballer who had beaten the Dodgers five times already that season. Maglie was called the Barber because he seemed to delight in knocking opposing hitters down. It must have worked. Maglie had a 23–6 season, the best year of his career.

The Dodgers went with Don Newcombe, a six-foot four-inch, 240-pound fastballer. "Newk," the first black man to pitch in the big leagues, was the Rookie of the Year in 1949. The next season he won 19 games, and he had a 20–9 record in 1951. He had beaten the Giants as many times as Maglie had beaten the Dodgers.

FIRST INNING. Brooklyn jumped out to a quick lead in the first inning. With one out, shortstop Pee Wee Reese walked. Duke Snider, playing center field, was up next. As a rookie, the Duke used to swing at a lot of bad pitches, so the Dodgers gave him an exercise. He had to stand at the plate and watch hundreds of pitches go by. He wasn't allowed to swing his bat. He just had to *say* if the pitches were strikes or balls. That's how he learned the strike zone. He learned it pretty well—Duke watched four of Maglie's pitches go by and took a walk to first base. Two runners on, one out.

Jackie Robinson, the man who courageously broke baseball's color barrier four years earlier, stepped up to the plate. He had hit .338 in the regular season. On the first pitch, he lined a single into left field. Pee Wee Reese scampered home, and the Dodgers were ahead 1–0.

People all over Brooklyn rejoiced. Maybe the Dodgers would put the game away early.

There was no further damage. Maglie, unshaven and

scowling, worked out of the jam by getting Andy Pafko, the Dodgers left fielder, to ground into a force play. First baseman Gil Hodges popped up to third.

Giants fans breathed a sigh of relief. Hodges was a real threat. He'd slugged 40 home runs that season, and the previous August he hit 4 in one game. Only three men had ever done that before (Lou Gehrig, Ed Delahanty, and Bobby Lowe).

The Giants didn't score in their half of the first inning. Don Newcombe was looking sharp.

SECOND INNING. But the Giants almost cracked the game open in the second. First baseman Whitey Lockman, who had been signed as a 16-year-old and hit a home run in his first major league at-bat, singled with one out. Then Bobby Thomson drove a Newcombe fastball down the left-field line.

Thomson was running with his head down and made it all the way to second. Unfortunately, he hadn't noticed that Lockman had *stopped* at second. Caught in a rundown, Thomson was tagged out by Jackie Robinson at second base. He ran off the field, embarrassed for having wrecked a rally in the most crucial game of his life. Willie Mays flied out to end the threat for the Giants.

At that point, the sky became more overcast and the lights in the Polo Grounds were flipped on. Somebody in the press box remarked that the lights had been turned on so Thomson would be able to see where he was going.

FIFTH INNING. Again in the fifth, the Giants threatened but could not score. Thomson hit a shot to left center and made it to second base (perhaps because there was nobody running in front of him). But he was stranded there when Mays fanned and Sal Maglie grounded out.

SEVENTH INNING. The score remained 1–0 in favor of Brooklyn until the seventh, when the fans began to realize that the whole season would be decided in the next few minutes. Giants left fielder Monte Irvin doubled to left. Whitey Lockman laid down a sacrifice bunt to advance Irvin to third. The Dodgers catcher, Rube Walker, pounced on the ball and threw it to third, but the throw was late. All hands were safe.

Players and fans wondered if Roy Campanella, the Dodgers' regular catcher, would have made the play. Campy had suffered a charley horse a few days earlier and was out for the series. His defense and bat (.325, 33 home runs) were sorely missed.

With runners at first and third, Bobby Thomson came up. Time was running out for the Giants. He was feeling the pressure of getting that tying run home. Newcombe got two strikes on him, but on the next pitch Thomson whacked a fly to center. It was deep enough. Irvin tagged up after the catch and ran home. The game was tied at 1–1. Both teams had played 156 baseball games in 1951, but the pennant would be decided in the next two innings.

EIGHTH INNING. After his problems in the first inning, Sal Maglie had been MAGnificent up until the eighth, when the roof caved in for the Giants.

Maglie struck out Carl "the Reading Rifle" Furillo, a .295 hitter, but Pee Wee Reese and Duke Snider both singled. Runners on first and third, one out. Maglie then bounced a curveball in the dirt, only his third wild pitch of the year. The ball rolled back to the screen and Reese came home. Dodgers 2, Giants 1. Snider made it all the way to third.

Leo Durocher instructed Maglie to walk Jackie Robinson intentionally. The slow-footed Andy Pafko was up next, and Leo was hoping to get him to ground into a double play.

It almost worked. Pafko slapped a bouncer toward Bobby Thomson at third. He tried to backhand the ball and step on the bag for a force play, but it ticked off Thomson's glove and dribbled into left field. Snider scored and the Dodgers now had a 3–1 lead. Jackie Robinson was on third now, and he was a man who wasn't afraid to steal home. Gil Hodges popped up for the second out of the inning.

Next, Dodgers third baseman Billy Cox drilled a bullet toward Thomson at third. He tried to get his body in front of it, but the ball shot by him. Thomson would say later that it was the hardest ball he had ever faced. Jackie Robinson scored on the hit and Brooklyn was up 4–1. Maglie retired Rube Walker to end the inning.

Having made one baserunning blunder and missed two ground balls at third base, Bobby Thomson was looking like the goat of the season.

IN THE BOTTOM OF THE EIGHTH, Don Newcombe sent the Giants down in order, striking out two of them. The Dodgers had a three-run lead, and they were three outs away from the World Series. It had been an incredible stretch run for the New York Giants, but now it looked like it was over.

A few disheartened fans headed for the Polo Ground exits. Yogi Berra, the Yankee catcher who once said "It ain't over till it's over," got up and left. He wanted to beat the traffic home.

NINTH INNING. Larry Jansen was brought in to relieve Sal Maglie. He sent the Dodgers down in order, and then it was the bottom of the ninth inning. The last chance for the Giants.

Leo Durocher gathered his team around him for a final, last ditch pep talk. "Fellows, you've done just a hell of a job all year long," he told them. "I'm proud of every one of you. We've got three whacks at them, boys! It's not over yet. Let's go out there and give them all we got, and let's leave this ball field, win or lose, with our heads in the air."

As Durocher ran out to his customary position in the third-base coaching box, second baseman Eddie Stanky shouted, "Let's win it for Leo!"

SO HERE WE ARE. Bottom of the ninth. Dodgers 4, Giants 1. Three more outs and the season would be over.

"I thought we were dead," recalled third baseman Bobby Thomson years later.

Don Newcombe was working on a four-hitter and looking unbeatable. But he was pitching for the fourth time in eight days, and he was dog tired.

"It's up to you to get it started," Durocher said to Giants captain Alvin Dark. Dark, a good contact hitter, carried his familiar black bat up to the plate.

The Giants yelled their battle cry from the dugout. "Let 'er rip! Let 'er rip!"

Newcombe got two quick strikes on Dark, but on the next pitch the scrappy shortstop pushed a skidding ground ball to the right side of the infield, between second baseman Jackie Robinson and first baseman Gil Hodges. Both men went for the ball, but it ticked off Hodges' glove into right field. Runner on first, nobody out.

Later, Dark would say, "If we didn't quit the last six weeks, we certainly weren't going to quit in the last inning of the last game."

Next up was Giants right fielder Don Mueller. He had the nickname Mandrake because he was a magician with a bat. It was said Mueller could actually *place* the ball just about anywhere he wanted to on the field.

Mueller noticed that Gil Hodges was playing close to the first-base bag to hold Dark on. That left most of the right side of the infield open. It probably wasn't the smartest defensive strategy for the Dodgers, because the Giants needed three runs just to *tie* the game. If Dark made it around the bases to score, it would only be 4–2. The Dodgers should have been concentrating on getting the *hitters* out, not holding Dark on at first.

Mueller saw a belt-high fastball from Newcombe and slapped a ground ball exactly where Hodges *should* have been playing. It could have been a double play. Instead, it went through the infield, and the Giants had runners on first and third with nobody out.

The tying run was at the plate in the person of Monte Irvin. He had led the National League with 121 RBIs that season, and he was looking for more.

This game wasn't over after all! Fans who had been heading for the exits quickly returned to their seats. Carl Erskine and Ralph Branca hurriedly began warming up in the Dodgers bullpen.

In his autobiography years later, Leo Durocher wrote that when Irvin stepped to the plate, he became "goose-pimply all over."

Jackie Robinson walked slowly to the pitcher's mound and whispered to Newcombe, "Two cheap hits. You're all right."

Newcombe's next pitch was a slider high and outside, but Irvin took a swing anyway and popped a foul outside of first base. Gil Hodges squeezed it for the first out. Irvin slammed his bat against the ground in disgust.

Next up was left-handed Whitey Lockman, a .282 hitter in 1951 and known as a good bad-ball hitter. Lockman fouled off Newcombe's first pitch, then took a cut at a high, outside fastball that was definitely off the plate. Somehow he made contact, and the ball whistled over Billy Cox's head at third, landed about a foot fair, and bounced around in the left-field corner. Alvin Dark scored, and it was now a 4–2 game. Mueller pulled safely into third and Lockman into second.

The tying run was now in scoring position, with just one out. The crowd at the Polo Grounds was going crazy.

In all the excitement, it took a few moments for anyone to realize that Don Mueller was on the ground at third base, writhing with pain. He had caught a cleat on the third-base bag and sprained his ankle severely. The Giants carried him off the field on a stretcher. Durocher sent in six-foot five-inch Clint "the Hondo Hurricane" Hartung to pinch-run.

Up to the plate stepped Bobby Thomson, whose accomplishments up until this point were to botch two grounders and get caught in a bonehead rundown.

QUICK RECAP: Bottom of the ninth. The score was 4–2 in favor of the Dodgers, but the Giants had men on second and third with one out. A single would tie the game. A home run would *win* the game . . . and the 1951 National League pennant.

CHARLIE DRESSEN, the Dodgers' manager, had two tough decisions to make. First base was open. He could intentionally walk Thomson to load the bases and pitch to Willie Mays. The rookie was in the on-deck circle, hoping and praying that the responsibility for winning or losing the pennant would not fall on his young shoulders.

With Thomson hitting .444 in the playoffs and Mays hitting .100, it made a lot of sense to walk Thomson and pitch to Mays. But Dressen had already decided against that strategy. He was the kind of manager who went by the book. Walking Thomson would put the winning run on base, and that's a big no-no in baseball.

Dressen's other decision to make was whether he should leave Don Newcombe in the game or bring in a relief pitcher. Newcombe was clearly pooped. Carl Erskine and Ralph Branca were loose in the bullpen.

The Dodgers held a conference on the mound, where Pee Wee Reese said to Dressen, "Charley, Newk has given us all he's got. Why don't you get somebody fresh in here?"

After thinking it over, Dressen agreed. He walked back to the dugout, picked up the telephone and barked, "Let me have Branca."

WHEN HE WAS JUST 17 years old, Ralph Branca had already had tryouts with three major league teams. He was signed by the Dodgers the following year. Branca threw *hard.* He became the youngest National League pitcher to win 20 games in a season in 1947, when he had a 21–12 record. The following year, he was hit on the leg by a line drive and developed an infection. In four years, his victories went from 21 to 14 to 13 to 7. In 1951, he was 13–12. His nickname was Honker—because he had a big nose.

Branca wasn't the luckiest pitcher in the world. He lost Game 1 of the 1947 World Series and Game 3 in 1949. He took a loss just two days earlier in the first game of the playoffs—by giving up a home run to Bobby Thomson.

He certainly wasn't superstitious. Branca wore number 13 on his uniform.

AS BRANCA WALKED in from the bullpen in left center-field, New York City looked like a scene from *The Day the Earth Stood Still.* There was no traffic in Manhattan. Cab drivers were turning down fares so they could pull over and listen to the radio. The tension was unbearable.

Branca arrived at the mound, where Charlie Dressen was waiting. The Dodgers manager flipped Branca the ball and gave the 25-year-old three words of advice: "Get him out."

LEO DUROCHER had a slightly longer conversation with Bobby Thomson. He told him to watch for fastballs high and tight. "Go ripping at it!" he said, "Get me a base hit here!"

Before he walked away, Durocher looked into Thomson's eyes and added seriously, "Bobby, if you ever hit one, hit one *now.*"

Twenty-seven-year-old Bobby Thomson was born in Glasgow, Scotland, and came to America when he was just two. He grew up on Staten Island and signed with the New York Giants (for $100 a month!) the day after his high-school graduation.

The Flying Scot, as he was called, was an ordinary hitter

with great speed and power. He hit 32 home runs that season, the most in his career.

THE DODGERS INFIELD offered Branca a few words of support. Before they went back to their positions, Branca cracked, "Anybody here got butterflies?"

As Thomson stepped up to the plate, the sun peeked through the clouds over the Polo Grounds for the first time all day.

"Wait and watch," Thomson said to himself. "Wait and watch."

Branca was concentrating so hard, he didn't hear the crowd. His plan was to set Thomson up for a curveball by throwing fastballs. Catcher Rube Walker squatted down for the first pitch. It was a fastball right down the middle and Thomson watched it go by for strike one.

The Giants groaned. Thomson could have *creamed* that pitch, and he wasn't likely to see another one so good. He stepped out of the batter's box and picked up a handful of dirt. He was behind in the count, 0–1.

Walker signaled for Branca to put the next pitch up and in, Thomson's weakness. The idea was to waste this pitch and drop the next pitch low and away. Branca went into his windup and threw the ball up and in, but Thomson lashed at it, a tomahawked uppercut.

Craaaaaaackkkkkk!

About ten million people stopped breathing. All eyes turned toward the 25-foot left-field wall.

It was a sinking drive close to the foul line. The ball looked like it might bounce off the wall for a double. The upper deck of the Polo Grounds hung over the lower deck, so it was just about impossible to hit a homer into the lower deck. The foul lines were short, less than 300 feet.

"Sink, sink, sink," prayed Branca.

Hartung and Lockman took off from third and second base. Thomson dropped the bat and headed for first. Left fielder Andy Pafko moved back, looking up, until his behind was against the wall.

On WMCA radio in New York, Russ Hodges's famous play-by-play sounded like this:

Branca is in his follow-through, Thomson swings, and the dotted line shows the path of baseball's most historic moment— *"the shot heard 'round the world" (NBL)*

"Branca throws. . . . There's a long drive. . . . It's gonna be . . . I believe . . ."

Then he paused for an instant before shouting: *"The Giants win the pennant! The Giants win the pennant! The Giants win the pennant! The Giants win the pennant! I don't believe it! I don't believe it! I don't believe it! Bobby Thomson hits into the lower deck of the left-field stands! The Giants win the pennant, and they're going crazy! Yaaayhooooo!!!"*

THE CROWD WAS STRANGELY SILENT for a moment, too stunned to realize what had happened. Then, spontaneously, the stadium exploded in a deafening roar. The ball had landed just inches over the wall.

Bobby Thomson jumped and skipped deliriously around the bases. (Later, he would tell reporters, "I didn't run around the bases—I rode around 'em on a cloud.") Eddie Stanky leaped up on Leo Durocher's back like a monkey.

Talk about clutch hitting! In one swing, the pennant changed hands and Thomson went from goat to hero.

Ralph Branca hung his head. Jackie Robinson stood at second base morosely, watching to see if Thomson touched all the bases. Thomson leaped the last ten feet and landed on the plate, where he was mobbed by the Giants.

"When my feet finally touched home plate and I saw my teammates' faces, that's when I realized I had won the pennant with one swing of the bat," Thomson told reporters after the game.

The television crew that had been waiting to capture the

Dodgers' victory celebration suddenly realized they were in the wrong clubhouse. They practically trampled Don Newcombe in their rush to move their equipment. Cases of champagne were furiously wheeled to the Giants' clubhouse.

Thomson was hoisted up on the shoulders of his teammates and carried around the field. Fans poured out of the stands to touch their heroes. When they closed in, the Giants put Thomson down, and he had to do some fancy open-field running to get to the clubhouse alive.

Car horns started tooting all over New York City, and Staten Island ferryboats blasted their whistles. (Bobby Thomson was living in Staten Island at the time.) The flow of phone calls surging across New York City was so heavy that lines had to be shut down.

Six young girls wearing Brooklyn jackets sat in the left-field bleachers weeping. The Dodgers' clubhouse was like a morgue. Branca was sprawled across steps crying and repeating the phrase, "Why me? Why me?"

The crowd refused to go home, chanting "We want Thomson!" "We want Maglie!" and "We want Stanky!" for half an hour. Finally, the victorious Giants appeared in a window in the Giants' clubhouse and waved to the crowd.

What Happened Afterward

Naturally, the press pressed Ralph Branca for his version of what came to be called the Shot Heard 'Round the World. "I made a decent pitch—up and in," Branca said. "I was trying to waste it on 0–1, then come back with a curveball low and away."

Bobby Thomson told reporters, "It wasn't a good pitch. It was high and inside, the kind they've been getting me out on all season. But I had to do something. I had messed things up pretty much earlier."

When asked how he felt, Thomson said, "It gave me the thrill of my life. I don't ever expect to hit another just like it. I'm going home and try to get a good night's sleep. The World Series starts tomorrow."

HOW COULD ANY WORLD SERIES possibly top the Giants/Dodgers playoff? The Giants were physically and emotionally exhausted after winning the pennant. They lost to the New York Yankees, four games to two. Bobby Thomson did not hit any home runs.

◆ The Dodgers would come back to win the National League pennant in 1952, 1953, 1955, and 1956. The Giants won in 1954.

◆ Six seasons after the Shot Heard 'Round the World, millions of devoted New York fans were heartbroken when both the Dodgers and Giants moved west and became the *Los Angeles* Dodgers and *San Francisco* Giants. The demand for a New York team in the National League caused the New York Mets to be born in 1962.

◆ After 25 years of being uncomfortable around each other, Ralph Branca and Bobby Thomson became friends. They could be seen together signing autographs, playing golf, and doing charity work. Their names will be linked in baseball lore forever.

For Baseball Trivia Lovers . . .

♦ The bat, glove, and spikes Bobby Thomson used on October 3, 1951, are in the Baseball Hall of Fame. The ball he hit for his home run is not.

The day after Thomson hit the home run, a fan walked up to him with a ball he claimed was *the* ball. The fan asked for two World Series tickets in exchange for it. When Thomson went into the clubhouse to get the tickets, he found a *dozen* baseballs at his locker, all delivered by fans claiming they'd caught the home run. It was impossible to tell if anyone was telling the truth.

A Baptist minister sitting in the left-field stands claimed he saw a young black boy catch the home run ball cleanly and dash out of the stands with it, but the boy (who would now be a middle-aged man) never came forward.

♦ The Dodgers got their name in the 1890s, when people who lived in Brooklyn were sometimes referred to as Trolley Dodgers.

♦ If you want to stump your grandfather, ask him to name the winning pitcher of the game. It was Larry Jansen, who retired three Dodgers in the ninth inning when it seemed so hopeless for the Giants. And if Grandpa gets *that* one right, ask him to name the plate umpire (Lou Jorda).

♦ Polo was never played at the Polo Grounds, which was located at 155th Street and Eighth Avenue in Manhattan.

The game was, however, played at another field nearby.

◆ When Willie Mays came to the Giants in 1951, he took over the center-field spot from Bobby Thomson, who moved to third base. Three years later, Thomson was playing for Milwaukee, and he broke his ankle. He was replaced by another future superstar—Henry Aaron.

◆ Hall of Famers who played in this game: Pee Wee Reese, Duke Snider, Jackie Robinson, Don Newcombe, Monte Irvin, Willie Mays. On the bench: Roy Campanella.

◆ Bobby Thomson's salary for 1951 was $24,000. After hitting the most famous home run in baseball history, he received a new contract that gave him a $2,000 raise.

◆ For the duration of the Giants' 16-game winning streak in 1951, Bobby Thomson wore the same pair of underwear. He was afraid the team would break the streak if he put on a different pair. He washed 'em, though.

◆ After Thomson's home run, sportswriter Red Smith titled his next column "Miracle of Coogan's Bluff," which became the name for the Giants' remarkable pennant drive. Coogan's Bluff was a hill outside the Polo Grounds.

In that column, Smith wrote, "The art of fiction is dead. Reality has strangled invention. Only the utterly impossible, the inexpressibly fantastic can ever be plausible again."

CHAPTER

2

The Fisk Game

THE DATE: Wednesday, October 22, 1975.
THE PLACE: Fenway Park, Boston.
THE SITUATION: Game 6 of the World Series
between the Boston Red Sox and
Cincinnati Reds. The Reds were leading
the Series three games to two.

Carlton Fisk waving the ball fair. (AP/Wide World Photos)

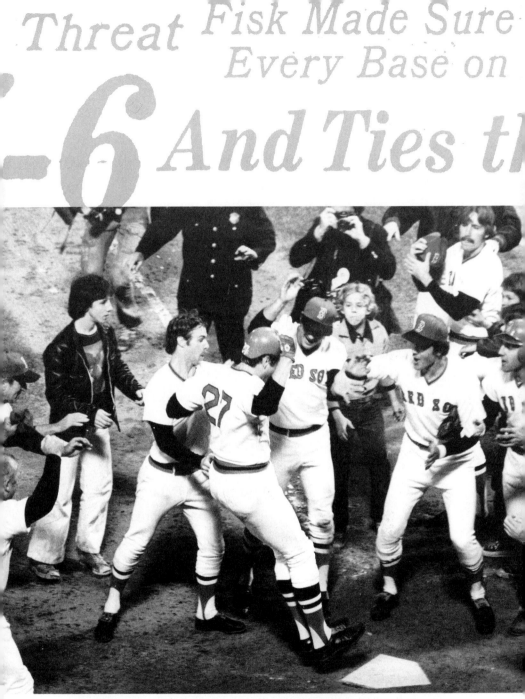

The ball was fair by about four inches. Fisk jumped and skipped and clapped his hands as he trotted around the bases like a kid running through a water sprinkler. (AP/Wide World Photos)

park seemed to become motionless.
Fisk stood watching, a few feet
from the plate. When he saw it hit,
he threw his bat in the air, jumped

*Y*OU CAN'T LOSE 'em all. Either the Boston Red Sox or the Cincinnati Reds were going to win the World Series in 1975. They were the only teams playing, and they couldn't *both* lose.

But before 1975, both of these teams were losers. The Reds—dubbed the Big Red Machine—hadn't won a World Championship in 35 years. In fact, they only won it *twice* in their 105-year history. And one of those World Series victories came in 1919, when the Chicago "Black Sox" lost *on purpose* for the benefit of gamblers.

After the team lost the Series in 1970 and 1972 and the National League playoff in 1973, people started saying the Big Red Machine had an automatic choke.

THE BOSTON RED SOX were even worse. They hadn't won a World Series in 57 years, since the days when their best pitcher *and* hitter was a kid named Babe Ruth. Like the Reds, the Red Sox had a history of blowing big games. They lost the seventh and final game of the World Series in 1946 and 1967. In 1948 they lost a one-game playoff to decide the pennant.

BUT THIS SEASON, Boston and Cincinnati dominated their respective leagues. The Red Sox finished four and a half games in front of the Baltimore Orioles and led the American League in runs and batting average (.275). Cincinnati put together the best record in baseball, winning

114 games. The second-place Los Angeles Dodgers were a distant twenty games behind when the season ended.

One of these teams would break its losing streak in the World Series, and the other would extend its streak of frustration.

The two teams battled it out through five nail-biting games, with the Reds winning three and the Sox two. Game 6 was a classic you-had-to-see-it-to-believe-it game that people will be talking about for decades.

Sports Illustrated wrote, "The sixth game of the 1975 Series will be the standard by which all future thrillers must be measured."

FIRST INNING. Even before he walked majestically to the mound, the Fenway crowd was chanting "LOO-EE! LOO-EE! LOO-EE!" When balding, overweight Luis Tiant appeared, the stadium exploded in cheers. Tiant, an exile from Cuba, was the hero of Boston, with 60 wins over the last three seasons. He'd had some back problems in 1975, but still won 18 games and led the Sox to the Eastern Division title.

So far in the post-season, Tiant had calmly shut down the powerful Oakland A's in Game 1 of the American League playoffs, shut out the Reds in Game 1 of the World Series, and beat them again in Game 4.

El Tiante threw a baffling assortment of pitches—knuckleballs, forkballs, screwballs, sliders—and he delivered them both sidearm and overhand. He could do everything but pitch behind his back. He was particularly hard to hit because he didn't look toward the plate at all during his delivery. When Tiant went into his windup, he would turn completely around to face *second base*. Then the ball would suddenly emerge against a background of elbows and knee-caps flying in every direction.

Tiant was working on a streak of 40 consecutive scoreless innings in Fenway Park. Three days of rain had given his 34-year-old right arm some needed rest.* He also drew inspiration from his father, a former pitching star in Cuba, sitting in the stands. One day in 1935, Luis Tiant, Sr., held Babe Ruth to a scratch single in two games. In 1975, it took a special agreement between Fidel Castro and the U.S. State Department to reunite the two Tiants for the first time in eight years.

El Tiante made it through the meat of the Reds' lineup in the first inning—Pete Rose, Ken Griffey, Joe Morgan, and Johnny Bench—without surrendering a run.

The starting pitcher for Cincinnati was Gary Nolan. Nolan was a control pitcher who had given up only 27 walks in 239 innings. He had missed the entire 1974 season because of shoulder problems, but came back to win 15 games in 1975. He started Game 3 and was knocked out after four innings.

The Baseball Encyclopedia lists Tiant's birthday as November 23, 1940, but many suspected he was born as much as five years earlier than that.

Nolan got the first two Red Sox out in the bottom of the first, but Carl Yastrzemski, nearing the end of his Hall of Fame career, lashed a 3–1 pitch to right for a single. Most of the fans didn't know that Yaz was playing with a handicap—the knowledge that his mother was dying from cancer and wasn't expected to live six months.

With Yastrzemski on first, Carlton Fisk, the Boston catcher who had hit .417 in the playoffs, bounced a 1–0 pitch through the left side of the infield. Runners on first and second, two out.

Next up was Fred Lynn, who was coming off one of the most spectacular rookie seasons in baseball history. By hitting .331 with 21 home runs and 105 RBIs, Lynn became the first player to win both the Rookie of the Year and Most Valuable Player awards. He also won a Gold Glove for his sparkling play in center field, and led the league in runs (103), slugging percentage (.556) and doubles (47). Lynn was superman in 1975.

He took ball one from Nolan and then drilled the next pitch over the Boston bullpen in right center for a towering three-run homer. Lynn clapped his hands once and motored around the bases.

Suddenly Luis Tiant had a nice cushion of runs to work with, and the Red Sox were on their way to evening up the World Series. Sox 3, Reds 0.

THIRD INNING. Sparky Anderson, the manager of the Reds, was called Captain Hook because he was so quick to yank his pitchers and bring in relievers. Gary Nolan was gone after two innings, replaced by left-hander Fred Norman, the loser in Game 4.

The Red Sox just about broke the game wide open against Norman in the third inning. Second baseman Denny Doyle started things off by doubling past first base with one out. Norman walked Carlton Fisk intentionally to set up a possible double play. But then he walked Fred Lynn *unintentionally*. The bases were loaded with two men out.

Sparky Anderson came out of the Cincinnati dugout and summoned Jack Billingham to pitch to third baseman Rico Petrocelli. Billingham, a distant relative of Hall of Famer Christy Mathewson, had become a footnote in baseball history when he gave up Hank Aaron's record-tying 714th home run.

Bringing him in at this stage was the right move. The three Boston runners were stranded when Billingham struck out Petrocelli with an outside curveball to end the inning. It was still 3–0, Red Sox.

FIFTH INNING. Luis Tiant, meanwhile, had been dodging bullets for four innings. It was only a matter of time before the Reds would figure out how to hit him. It happened in the fifth inning. With one out, Tiant walked Ed Armbrister, who was pinch-hitting for Billingham. Pete Rose (.317 for the year) was up next, and he lined a hard single to center on a 3–2 pitch. Runners on first and third, one out.

Ken Griffey, a .305 hitter during the regular season, came to the plate. On a 2–2 count, Griffey launched a cannon shot to straightaway center.

Fred Lynn raced back and to his left. At the last instant, Lynn leaped against the concrete barrier. Man and ball hit the wall at about the same moment and then went their separate ways. Lynn came down hard and slumped to the dirt like an old puppet.

The ball bounded away. Armbrister and Rose scored. Griffey slid into third safely. Now it was a one-run ball game. Sox 3, Reds 2.

Fred Lynn lay on the warning track for five minutes, with a hush enveloping Fenway Park. If you ever rent the highlight film to this World Series (and you should), you'll hear Lynn finally mumble to the Red Sox trainer, "I'll be okay" before clumsily struggling to his feet. Bravely, Lynn stayed in the game.

The Reds weren't finished. Johnny Bench, who had slugged 28 home runs and driven in 110 runs during the season, stepped up to the plate. He'd already struck out twice, but this time he drilled Tiant's first pitch deep to left field.

In quirky Fenway Park, they call the left-field wall the Green Monster. It's only 315 feet down the foul line, but the wall is 40 feet high. It has turned many a routine fly ball into a double and many a double into a single.

Carl Yastrzemski, who had been playing in front of the Monster for 15 seasons, played the carom perfectly and whipped the ball into second to hold Bench to a long single.

But Ken Griffey jogged home from third to tie the game up. Sox 3, Reds 3. Tiant struck out Tony Perez to stop the bleeding.

Clay Carroll shot down the Sox in the bottom of the fifth, and there was no scoring in the sixth.

SEVENTH INNING. After watching Luis Tiant for 25 innings, the Reds had his number. Ken Griffey singled wide of first, and Joe Morgan punched an opposite-field single to left field. Runners on first and second, nobody out. Tiant got Johnny Bench on a short fly to left field and Tony Perez on a fly to right. Griffey tagged up after the catch and made it to third.

Next up was big George Foster, who had hit .300 and 23 home runs that year. Foster slammed a line drive all the way to the center-field fence 400 feet away. It went for a double, and by the time Fred Lynn had relayed the ball in, Griffey and Morgan had scooted around to score. Reds 5, Sox 3. Even Luis Tiant fans began to wish Red Sox manager Darrell Johnson would bring in a reliever.

EIGHTH INNING. Things got worse for Boston in the top of the eighth, when Cincinnati center fielder Cesar Geronimo (is that a great baseball name, or what?) led off and sent Tiant's first pitch sailing into the right-field stands for his second home run of the World Series.

The score was now Reds 6, Sox 3, and it looked like the season was over for Boston.

That was enough. Darrell Johnson came in to give Tiant

the hook. As the old master walked off the mound, Fenway fans erupted with a standing ovation. Tiant was replaced by Roger Moret, a lefty from Puerto Rico who chewed a big wad of bubble gum while he pitched. Moret (14–3) put out the fire. But Boston was three runs down, and there were just six outs remaining in the game.

PEDRO BORBON was on the mound for the Reds in the bottom of the eighth, Cincinnati's fifth pitcher of the game. Fred Lynn smashed a shot off Borbon's leg, and was safe at first when the ball bounced away. Borbon may have been feeling the sting, because he walked Rico Petrocelli to put runners at first and second with nobody out.

Sparky Anderson rushed out to replace Borbon with the Reds' *sixth* pitcher of the night, Rawly Eastwick. A rookie with 22 saves on the year, Eastwick was the winner for Cincinnati in Game 2 and Game 3.

The tying run was at the plate, in the name of Dwight Evans. Evans was a third-year man who had all the markings of a superstar, but two serious beanings had left him merely a solid hitter and eight-time Gold Glove winner. In Game 3, he had hit a two-run homer in the ninth that sent the game into extra innings. The pitcher—Rawly Eastwick.

This time Eastwick struck out Evans on fastballs. One out. Rick Burleson, the Red Sox shortstop, flied out to shallow left field. Two outs. Now the Reds were four outs away from the world championship.

The crowd cheered as left-hander Bernie Carbo stepped

in to pinch-hit for Roger Moret. Carbo, who started his career as a Cincinnati Red, was a character who carried a stuffed gorilla named Mighty Joe Young on the road with him. He had a reputation for having nerves of steel, which is what a pinch hitter needs. Carbo hit three pinch-hit homers during the season. The Fenway crowd remembered his last at bat, in Game 3—also a homer.

Eastwick got two strikes on Carbo, then wasted two pitches trying to get him to swing at a bad ball. With the count 2–2, Eastwick went to his slider. Carbo was looking for a fastball and was totally fooled, but took an awkward swing and managed to foul the ball off to the left. Baseball writer Roger Angell wrote that Carbo looked "like someone fighting off a wasp with a croquet mallet."

Bench and Eastwick figured Carbo would be expecting the same pitch again, so they decided to cross him up with a fastball. Bad move. The pitch was high, over the plate, and Carbo slammed it 400 feet into the center-field bleachers. Three-run homer!

Bedlam in Fenway Park! Carbo danced around the bases behind Lynn and Petrocelli, and the rest of the Red Sox mobbed them at the plate. Carbo had tied a World Series record for pinch-hit homers set in 1959 by Chuck Essegian of the Dodgers. More importantly, he had tied the game. Sox 6, Reds 6.

"I was telling myself not to strike out," Carbo told reporters after the game. "I was just trying to put the ball in play someplace."

"It was just a terrible pitch," said Eastwick. "A high fastball. With two strikes, I just wanted to get it in on him, but it was out and up."

NINTH INNING. The Reds went down in order in the top of the ninth, and the Sox had a golden opportunity to put the game away. Eastwick, still on the mound, walked Denny Doyle. Yastrzemski singled to right on an 0–2 pitch, sending Doyle to third and Eastwick to the showers. Left-hander Will McEnaney was brought in to intentionally walk Carlton Fisk.

So here we are. Bottom of the ninth. Tie game. Bases loaded. Nobody out. Fred Lynn, the superman of the year, was at the plate. Now it was Cincinnati with its back against the wall. Boston's winning run—Denny Doyle—was just 90 feet away.

Lynn hit a fly ball to left. It wasn't deep, about halfway between third base and the Green Monster. George Foster camped under it.

Third-base coaches, for the most part, stand around and shout encouragement to their runners. But this is one situation in which they play a crucial part in the ballgame. On a fly ball with nobody out, the runner at third has a choice—he can tag up and try to score after the catch, or stay put and hope the next guy up gets a hit.

If the fly ball is hit deep, just about anybody can score from third. If the ball is hit to the shallow outfield, it's riskier to try for home. And if the outfielder has a great arm, it's riskier still. The third-base coach has the responsibility to make that decision for the runner and tell him what to do.

As the ball was coming down, third-base coach Don Zimmer shouted to Denny Doyle, "No! No! No!" Zimmer didn't feel the ball had been hit deep enough for Doyle to tag up and score.

But in the excitement, Doyle thought Zimmer was saying, "Go! Go! Go!" The instant left fielder George Foster caught the ball, Doyle took off for home.

He was meat. Foster uncorked a perfect one-hop throw to the plate. Johnny Bench put his patented one-hand glove tag on Doyle. Double play. The game goes on.

If Doyle had stayed at third, Boston would have had the bases loaded with one out. Instead, they had runners on first and second with *two* outs.

When Rico Petrocelli grounded out to third, the Fenway faithful let out a groan that could be heard all over New England. If the Red Sox couldn't score with the bases loaded and nobody out, how *could* they score?

The game went into extra innings.

ELEVENTH INNING. When the tenth inning ended with the game still deadlocked, everybody in the ballpark realized they were watching something special. First the Sox had a three-run lead, then the Reds tied it up. Then the *Reds* had a three-run lead, and the *Sox* tied it up. Both teams had blown opportunities to put the game out of reach.

Before Pete Rose stepped into the batter's box to start the eleventh, he turned to Boston catcher Carlton Fisk.

"This is some kind of game, isn't it?" Rose said.

"Some kind of game," agreed Fisk.

Dick Drago, the ace of the Boston bullpen with 15 saves, was now in the game. He had been the losing pitcher of Game 2. Drago nicked Rose with a pitch, and Charlie Hustle sprinted down to first base, as was his custom.

Ken Griffey was the next batter. He dropped down a bunt to sacrifice Rose to second, but Fisk, in a daring play, grabbed the ball and whipped a perfect peg to nail Rose. Griffey was safe at first.

Joe Morgan stepped in. Morgan was a small man—five feet seven inches, 160 pounds, but a dynamo on a baseball diamond. His .327 average, 94 RBIs, 67 steals, and league-leading 132 walks made him the National League MVP in 1975. (He would win it again the next season.) Only two men in baseball history had more walks than Joe Morgan— Babe Ruth and Ted Williams.

Morgan had an odd habit when he batted. He would flap his left arm repeatedly as he waited for each pitch, like he was pumping himself up to swing the bat. He looked a little bit like a penguin.

After a few good flaps, Morgan took a cut at a Drago offering and rocketed a line drive to right. The ball was heading for the wall, or maybe over it. We'll never know for sure.

Dwight Evans, the Boston right fielder, started running

back and to his right the instant the ball left the bat. Going full speed, a stride from the wall, Evans stabbed his glove up almost blindly. Miraculously, the ball stuck in the webbing. Evans slammed into the low wall and held on.

As if that wasn't spectacular enough, Evans bounced off the wall, whirled, and threw the ball back to the infield. Yastrzemski grabbed the relay and tossed it to Burleson covering first. The base runner, Ken Griffey, was out by about a mile and a half.

What could have been a game-winning home run had been turned into a double play. After the game, Sparky Anderson would say Evans's catch was one of the greatest he'd ever seen.

Pat Darcy came in and retired Boston in order in the eleventh. Darcy was the eighth pitcher for the Reds and twelfth pitcher in the game, a World Series record.

TWELFTH INNING. Rick Wise, who topped the Red Sox pitchers with 19 wins in 1975, held the Reds scoreless in the top of the twelfth.

It was now past midnight on the East Coast. The marathon game had been going on for four hours and one minute. Both teams had just about run out of pitchers. Chances were the next club to score would win the game. Boston was the home team, so if it could get a run home the game would instantly be over.

Twenty-seven-year-old Carlton Fisk led off the inning for the Red Sox. "Pudge," as he was affectionately known, was

a native New England boy (from Vermont) who was particularly loved by Boston fans. His career was almost ended
by a knee injury the previous year, and he broke his arm
during spring training. But he came back to hit .331 the
second half of the season and .417 in the American League
playoffs. He hit a home run in Game 3 of the Series.

So far in this game, Fisk had singled, grounded out twice,
and was walked intentionally twice. Darcy kicked his leg
up and zipped in his first pitch. Fisk let it go by. High, ball
one.

Johnny Bench signaled for a sinker down and in. A good
catcher knows to move the ball around and keep hitters off
balance. Darcy put it where he wanted it, but this time Fisk
pulled the trigger and he made contact.

The ball sailed off on a high arc into the dark Boston sky.
Above the lights of Fenway Park, it was out of sight, like a
spaceship temporarily out of radio contact with Mission
Control.

Fisk took a step toward first and stopped to watch the
path of the ball. 35,000 people in Fenway Park stopped
munching their peanuts and Cracker Jacks to watch the
path of the ball. Sixty-two million TV viewers, many of
them awake long after bedtime, stopped to watch the path
of the ball.

The whole world, it seemed, stopped to watch the path
of the ball.

It clearly had the distance and height to make it over the
Green Monster, but did it have the direction? Fisk had

pulled it perilously close to the foul line, and it was curving to the left.

Thanks to the miracle of videotape and some excellent NBC camerawork, this is one of the most memorable moments in World Series history—Carlton Fisk waving his arms to urge the ball fair, like a hula dancer or some demented air traffic controller.

After what seemed like an eternity, the ball reappeared from the heavens. There was a moment of indecision, and then it ricocheted off the yellow foul pole. Umpire Dick Stello signaled it was a fair ball—by about four inches.

Home run! That was the ball game! Sox 7, Reds 6.

Fisk thrust his hands up, threw his bat in the air and leaped with joy. He jumped and skipped and clapped his hands as he trotted around the bases like a kid running through a water sprinkler.

The Fenway Park organist launched into Handel's *Hallelujah Chorus*. Church bells in Boston began to peal.

Fans were streaming onto the field as Fisk made his way around the bases. As he rounded third, a man in blue jeans slapped hands with him.

"I made sure I touched every base," Fisk would say later. "Even if I had to straight-arm people or knock them down, I made sure I touched every bit of white I saw out there."

Finally, Fisk jumped on home plate with both feet. The Sox mauled him there. The scene looked like the Red Sox had won the World Series, though all they had done was tie it up at three games apiece.

As Red Sox shortstop Rick Burleson ran to the plate to congratulate Carlton Fisk, he told teammate Rick Miller, "We just might have won the greatest game ever played."

What Happened Afterward

Carlton Fisk's comments in the locker room: "He's a lowball pitcher, I'm a lowball, dead-pull hitter, so I was looking for that one pitch in that one area. I got it, then drove it. I knew it was going to be foul or a home run. I don't think I've ever gone through a more emotional game."

The next day the World Series was decided in Game 7. Boston's euphoria didn't carry over. They had a 3–0 lead in the third inning, but Cincinnati showed a lot of guts and came back to win it in the ninth on a two-out bloop single by Joe Morgan.

The Reds' hard luck history was over. They won the World Series the next year, too, and again in 1990.

Boston's hard luck history continued after 1975. They lost a one-game playoff to decide the American League pennant in 1978. In 1986 they were one strike away from winning the World Series, when a ground ball went through the legs of first baseman Bill Buckner. The Sox lost the game, and the next day they lost the deciding seventh game of the Series to the New York Mets.

As of 1993, it is three-quarters of a century since the Red Sox last won the World Series.

◆ Eighteen years later, the hero of the game, Carlton Fisk, was still an active player. Fisk is one of the few players (and one of the *very* few catchers) to have played in the majors in four different decades. He barely made it, by coming to the plate just five times (and getting no hits) in two 1969 games.

At the end of the 1992 season, Fisk had a lifetime average of .270, with 375 home runs, 1326 RBIs, 2346 hits, 421 doubles, 47 triples, and 128 stolen bases. He had caught more games and hit more home runs than any catcher in baseball history. Fisk retired in the middle of 1993. He is a sure Hall of Famer.

♦ A few weeks after the 1975 World Series, an arbiter ruled that pitchers Andy Messersmith (of the Dodgers) and Dave McNally (of the Expos) were free agents. This decision put an end to baseball's 100-year-old "reserve clause," which bound players to their teams, and started the era of free agency.

For Baseball Trivia Lovers . . .

♦ Here's a trivia question that's sure to stump just about anybody: name *two* four-decade men who played for Boston in 1975.

The second one is TV broadcaster Tim McCarver, who was *also* a catcher. McCarver (1959–1980) played just 12 games for the Red Sox that season, but he got 8 hits in 21 at bats—a .381 average.

♦ The 1975 World Series is widely regarded as one of the best ever. Five of the games were decided by one run. Two were decided in the last inning, and two went into extra innings. In six of the seven games, the winning team came from behind *twice*. Boston led in all seven games and lost the lead in five of them.

◆ Carl Yastrzemski made the last out in the 1975 World Series. He had also made the last out in the 1967 World Series *and* the 1978 American League playoff.

Yaz played 23 years for the Red Sox, which is longer than anybody else ever played for one team. He never played for a World Series winner. When he retired he had played 3,308 games, second on the all-time list. He was third in at-bats, fourth in walks, sixth in hits and doubles, and ninth in RBIs. He's the only American Leaguer to collect both 3,000 hits and 400 home runs.

◆ Luis Tiant pitched a shutout in his first big-league game, and in 1966 he pitched four of them in a row. He once struck out 19 batters in a ten-inning game. In 1968, Tiant had a 21–9 record for Cleveland. The very next season, his record was 9–20.

◆ The first two cities to have professional baseball teams back in the 1800s were Boston and Cincinnati.

◆ How's this for consistency? From 1982 to 1988, these were Fred Lynn's home-run totals: 21, 22, 23, 23, 23, 23, 25. Also, he hit 21 in 1975 and 23 in 1978.

Lynn was touted to be the next Joe DiMaggio, but after five great seasons with the Red Sox, he hurt an ankle sliding into second base and was never the same again. He still played 16 years in the big leagues, with a .283 career average, 306 home runs, 1,111 RBIs, 388 doubles, and 43 triples. In 1979 he led the American League, hitting .333. In 1983 he hit the only grand slam home run in the history of the All-Star Game.

♦ Hall of Famers who played in this game: Joe Morgan, Johnny Bench, Carl Yastrzemski.

♦ The winning pitcher of the game was Rick Wise, even though he gave up two hits in one inning of relief. Wise owns a piece of major-league history. On June 23, 1971, he became the only player to pitch a no-hitter and hit two home runs in the game as well.

♦ When Fenway Park was built in 1912, a home run over the left-field fence was considered an impossibility. They were playing with a "dead ball" in those days. The first man to hit one out was Hugh Bradley, that same year. Bradley would hit just one more homer in his five-year career.

Fenway has only a few feet of foul territory between the field and the fans. It seats fewer people than any other major league stadium—34,000. Many seats are closer to home plate than the infielders are.

♦ Sparky Anderson was the first manager to win 600 games in each league, and the first manager to win a World Series in each league. As a player, he lasted just one season, hitting .218 for the Phillies in 1959.

♦ Ken Griffey came from Donora, Pennsylvania, the same hometown as Hall of Famer Stan Musial. In 1989, Griffey made baseball history by playing at the same time as his son, Ken Griffey, Jr.

CHAPTER
3
The Haddix Game

THE DATE: Tuesday, May 26, 1959.
THE PLACE: County Stadium, Milwaukee.
THE SITUATION: Mid-season game between the Milwaukee Braves and Pittsburgh Pirates.

Harvey Haddix (George Brace)

homer in a pinch-
night to give the
Giants a 6-4 vic-
os Angeles.

Haddix in action during the fateful game. Win or lose,
he pitched the greatest game in baseball history. (NBL)

ey Haddix | praise mounted, the dust settled
d as the | around the thirteenth inning in

on, Then Confusion

*N*O HITS. NO RUNS. NO ERRORS. No walks. No base runners.

That pretty much sums up what a perfect game is. Before Harvey Haddix took the mound on May 26, 1959, there had been just seven perfect games in baseball history.

Back in 1880, John Lee Richmond and John Montgomery Ward pitched perfect games within five days of each other. Hall of Famer Cy Young had one in 1904, Addie Joss in 1908, Ernie Shore in 1917, Charlie Robertson in 1922, and Don Larsen pitched one in the 1956 World Series.

That's *it*.

This is the story of the night Harvey Haddix pitched the greatest game in baseball history . . . and *lost*.

HADDIX, A COUNTRY BOY from Medway, Ohio, was called the Kitten because he looked like Harry Brecheen, a pitcher known as the Cat. Brecheen and Haddix were the one-two punch for the Cardinals in 1952. That was the year Harvey broke into the big leagues at age 27. He was a five foot nine inch left-hander, a curveball specialist with excellent control.

In his first full season, Haddix sported a sensational 20–9 record, with a league-leading six shutouts. The next year he was 18–13.

It was downhill after that, and by 1959 he had bounced around to four teams in four seasons. He landed with the Pittsburgh Pirates that season in a trade with Cincinnati, where he'd won eight games and lost seven.

The Pirates arrived in Milwaukee on Tuesday for a series with the first place Braves. Pittsburgh was in third place, three and a half games back. A win that night would keep them right in the thick of the pennant race.

Haddix was feeling lousy and felt like he might have the flu, so he went to bed as soon as he checked into the team hotel. Unfortunately, he was scheduled to be the starting pitcher that night, so he dragged himself out of bed and made it to the ballpark by game time.

He would have his work cut out for him. Harvey had lost his last four games against Milwaukee, a team of sluggers. Eddie Mathews was on his way to hitting 46 home runs for the Braves that season, and Hank Aaron (39), Joe Adcock (25), and Del Crandall (21) were also long-ball threats. Aaron was tearing up the league, and would finish the season hitting .355, his highest average ever.

IN THE PIRATES' LOCKER ROOM, Haddix sat down wearily and told his teammates how he intended to pitch to each of the Braves batters.

"Harv," said third baseman Don Hoak, "if you pitch the way you say you will, you'll have a no-hitter."

If Hoak only knew.

To make things even tougher for Haddix, the Braves were going with their best that night. Right-hander Lew Burdette would be on the mound. He was already 7–2 and on his way to a 21-victory season, the most in his career. Haddix had a less impressive 3–2 record.

FIRST INNING. It was a warm and muggy night. The clouds looked threatening at game time, and there were flashes of lightning in the distant sky. County Stadium was known as a good hitter's park, but it wouldn't be tonight. Maybe it was a taste of things to come when both Lew Burdette and Harvey Haddix retired the side 1–2–3.

SECOND INNING. Pittsburgh first baseman Rocky Nelson led off with a single to right field but was wiped out on a double-play grounder off the bat of left fielder Bob Skinner.

In the bottom of the second, Haddix struck out Milwaukee first baseman Joe Adcock. He got Wes Covington and Del Crandall on routine ground balls. Getting the first six batters out in a game doesn't mean much, and nobody paid much attention to it at the time.

THIRD INNING. The Pirates mounted their first big threat. Don Hoak singled to left. Roman Mejias, filling in at right field for the injured Roberto Clemente, bounced to second. Hoak was forced out, leaving Mejias on first. Haddix came up and ripped a line drive straight at Burdette. The ball ricocheted off the pitcher's leg and rolled a few feet toward second.

That should have put runners at first and second, but Mejias decided to gamble and try for third. Milwaukee shortstop Johnny Logan ran in, scooped up the ball, wheeled, and nailed Mejias by ten feet.

That baserunning blunder would come back to haunt the Pirates, and especially Harvey Haddix. Because the next batter, shortstop Dick Schofield, singled. If Mejias hadn't tried to go from first to third on Haddix's infield single, he would have scored easily.

Bill Virdon flied out to end the inning, stranding Haddix and Schofield on the bases. The Pirates had made three hits in the inning, but could not push across a run.

MEANWHILE, HARVEY HADDIX was showing no flu symptoms whatsoever. He was using his fastball effectively and nipping the corners at will with his curve. In the bottom of the third, he came the closest to giving up a hit when Johnny Logan whacked a line drive that Dick Schofield had to leap up and grab at short.

As he walked off the mound, Haddix could see the big zero on the scoreboard indicating the number of hits Milwaukee had made. It occurred to him that he was working on a no-hitter, even though it was still quite early in the game.

It's a longtime baseball tradition that players, broadcasters, and fans *never* mention a no-hitter until it's over. To talk about a no-hitter in progress is to jinx it. When Haddix got the third out in the third inning, Pirate radio announcer Bob Prince simply told his listeners, "First nine men up and down." There was no way he was going to say that Harvey Haddix was in the middle of a perfect, no-hit game.

FIFTH INNING. Roman Mejias singled again for the Pirates, but he was wiped off the bases when Haddix bounced into a double play. Lew Burdette was having a good night, too, allowing a few harmless singles but otherwise mowing down the Pirates almost as easily as Haddix was mowing down the Braves.

During most games, Pirates relief ace Elroy Face would make his way to the bullpen around the fifth inning in case he would be needed near the end of the game. Not today.

"None of us moved," Face said later. "We just stayed and enjoyed it."

By this time, word was buzzing through the crowd that they were witnessing a perfect game in the works. A light rain began to fall and a few fair-weather fans left their seats.

SIXTH INNING. Both Burdette and Haddix sent the hitters down in order. When Haddix got the final out, Bob Prince told the radio audience cryptically, "Haddix has zeroed the board."

AT FIRST GLANCE, perfect games aren't that exciting to watch. It's more interesting to see hitters slamming the ball all over the ballpark and runners racing around the bases than it is to see them striking out, popping up, and hitting easy grounders.

What's exciting about a no-hitter or a perfect game is seeing if the pitcher can pull it off. How long can he keep it up? A single pitch in the wrong spot, a bad hop, or a lucky hit can end it at any moment.

Will the pitcher go into the record books and be remembered forever, or will he blow it? Can he take the mounting pressure as the innings go by? *That's* dramatic, and that's why no-hitters and perfect games become more intense with every inning.

SEVENTH INNING. Once again, the Pirates threatened but could not score. Bob Skinner hit a shot to right center that looked like it was over the wall. But the wind held it up and center fielder Andy Pafko caught it against the fence.

It was drizzling steadily now, but Haddix calmly got Hall of Famers Henry Aaron and Eddie Mathews on a ground out and strikeout. It was clear to anyone who knew anything about baseball that Harvey Haddix was pitching the game of his life.

The game of *anybody's* life.

EIGHTH INNING. Once again, it was three up and three down for both pitchers. After Haddix got the third out, Bob Prince told his listeners, "Don't go away. We are on the verge of baseball history."

NINTH INNING. It doesn't matter *how* great a game you're pitching if your teammates can't score. As Dick Schofield stepped up to the plate, leading off the ninth, the

Pittsburgh bench was shouting, "Come on, let's get Harvey a run!"

Schofield made an out, but Bill Virdon responded with a single to center. Smoky Burgess, the Pirate catcher, flied out, but Rocky Nelson singled to right. Virdon advanced to third.

Runners at first and third, two outs. This was a real chance to score, and at a time the Pirates needed it.

But Bob Skinner hit a grounder to first. Joe Adcock was right there and made the play unassisted for the third out. Lew Burdette had given up eight hits through the first nine innings, but he hadn't walked a single batter, and he hadn't allowed a run.

Haddix knew he needed just three more outs for his no-hitter, and he didn't want to let it slip away. As a rookie with the St. Louis Cardinals in 1953, he'd had a no-hitter through eight innings of a game against the Phillies. It was spoiled when Richie Ashburn singled to lead off the ninth.

If Haddix was tiring, he wasn't showing it. He struck out Andy Pafko and got Johnny Logan on a lazy fly to left field.

With two out in the bottom of the ninth, it was Lew Burdette's turn to hit. Braves manager Fred Haney could have sent in a pinch hitter, who would certainly have a better chance of getting a hit than Burdette (.183 lifetime). But with the game still scoreless, and with Burdette pitching so well, Haney decided to leave his pitcher in the game.

When Burdette swung and missed at strike three, Bob Prince shouted into his microphone, "Harvey Haddix has pitched a perfect, no-hit, no-run game!" The Milwaukee crowd gave Haddix a hand as he came to the bench, and the Pirates mobbed him.

It had been a remarkable performance. Not one Brave had reached first base. Only two balls had been hit out of the infield. Haddix had only thrown 78 pitches in nine innings.

Of course, none of that meant a thing in the standings. At the end of nine innings, the score was Braves 0, Pirates 0. The game would be decided in extra innings.

None of the other seven perfect games in baseball history went past nine innings. The longest no-hitter was pitched way back in 1884 by Sam Kimber of Brooklyn. Kimber's game was called at 0–0 after 11 innings because of darkness.

TENTH INNING. Now it was an endurance contest. How long could Haddix and Burdette keep going? One of the two pitchers would eventually crack. It was only a matter of time. Nobody in the Pittsburgh or Milwaukee dugout would sit down for the rest of the game. It was too tense.

With one out in the tenth inning, Don Hoak singled for the Pirates. Pinch hitter Dick Stuart hit a drive that looked like it might be out of there, but the wind held it up, and Andy Pafko caught it at the warning track.

Even the Braves were observing the baseball tradition of not mentioning the perfect game. When Harvey Haddix stepped to the plate to bat, Milwaukee catcher Del Crandall told him, "Say, you're pitching a pretty good game." That was the understatement of the year.

Once again, the Pirates could not score.

HADDIX WAS STARTING TO TIRE, and it showed. Braves pinch hitter Del Rice and Eddie Mathews each drove balls to the center-field wall, but they were caught by the sure-handed Bill Virdon. Hank Aaron grounded to short, and Haddix's game was still perfect through ten innings.

ELEVENTH INNING. Dick Schofield singled off Burdette's hand to lead off the inning for the Pirates, but Virdon bounced into a force play, and Burgess bounced into a double play. Another goose egg for Pittsburgh.

Haddix was frustrated and struggling now, getting hitters out on guts and luck. Adcock grounded out to short. Wes Covington and Del Crandall hit towering drives to center that were caught at the fence by Virdon. When he recorded the third out, Haddix was the author of the longest no-hitter in baseball history.

He knew he was working on a no-hitter since the third inning, but he didn't realize it was a perfect game as well. "I thought perhaps I might have walked somebody in the early innings," he said after the game. "But going down the stretch, my main idea was to win. We needed this one badly to keep going."

TWELFTH INNING. With two outs, Pirates second baseman Bill Mazeroski singled. But Don Hoak bounced into a force play to choke off another Pittsburgh threat.

Once again, Haddix sent the side down in order. The last Braves batter in the inning was Lew Burdette, and the fans gave him a hand as he stepped to the plate. He grounded to third.

Haddix, who was not exactly one of baseball's premiere pitchers, had pitched the best 12 innings in baseball history. Everyone in County Stadium was wondering how much longer he could go on.

THIRTEENTH INNING. By now, Haddix and Burdette were two very tired pitchers. They were like a pair of heavyweight boxers in the fifteenth round of a tough fight, still on their feet, but staggering. The human body isn't *designed* to throw a baseball so hard for so long.

Burdette got the first two Pirates out, and then Schofield singled. It was his third hit of the night, and the twelfth for the Pirates. But once again, Burdette reached back for a little extra. He got Bill Virdon on a ground out to shut out the Pirates for the thirteenth straight inning.

IMAGINE HOW FRUSTRATING it must have been for Harvey Haddix. He had retired 36 batters in a row within a single game, a feat no pitcher had ever accomplished before (or since). There had been no hard hit balls. He had only thrown 104 pitches in 12 innings, and never more than

14 in a single inning. He had not been behind in the count to a batter all night.

And yet, all he had to show for his work was a scoreless tie.

Before he left the dugout to pitch the thirteenth inning, Pirates manager Danny Murtaugh gently suggested to Haddix that maybe he should call it a night. But Harvey refused to come out of the game. He was going to stick it out until the end.

Murtaugh didn't force the issue. When a man is making history, you have to let events run their course. If Haddix had been taken out, baseball fans would have argued for centuries about how long the perfect game would have lasted if he'd hung in there.

The first Milwaukee batter in the thirteenth was Felix Mantilla, a right-handed speedster. Haddix got two strikes on him. On the next pitch, he thought he had the strikeout, but umpire Vinnie Smith called the pitch a ball.

Mantilla then hit a routine grounder to third. Don Hoak picked it up cleanly and carefully threw to first. Maybe *too* carefully. The ball hit the dirt before it reached first baseman Rocky Nelson. Nelson couldn't make the scoop and Mantilla was safe.

The perfect game was gone.

The Pirates argued that Mantilla had rounded first base toward second and had been tagged out, but the umpires could not be convinced. The play was ruled an error on Hoak.

While Haddix no longer had a perfect game, he still had a no-hitter.

But there was a runner on first—the Braves' first base runner of the whole game—with nobody out. It was an obvious sacrifice situation. Eddie Mathews bunted the ball, and Haddix threw him out at first. Mantilla advanced to second.

Runner at second, one out. Slugger Hank Aaron, who would go on to hit more home runs than any man to ever play the game, stepped up to the plate.

Haddix had been pitching so well, Pirates manager Danny Murtaugh hadn't had to make many tough decisions up until this point. Now he had to decide if Haddix should pitch to Aaron or walk him intentionally and pitch to Joe Adcock. First base was open. Aaron and Adcock were both right-handed hitters.

Murtaugh decided to walk Aaron. As mentioned previously, Aaron was having the best year of his career. Besides, if Aaron came around to score, it wouldn't mean anything anyway because the game would be over if Mantilla scored from second.

The crowd, which had been rooting for Haddix to make history, suddenly realized their hometown Braves were in a position to win the game. A cheer went up as Adcock stepped to the plate.

Haddix had already struck Adcock out twice and got him twice on ground balls, mostly by throwing sliders away from the plate. A good hitter will eventually figure out how to hit a tough pitch, and Adcock was a good hitter. During a game against the Dodgers in 1954, he slammed four home runs and a double. Here, he took ball one outside.

On the next pitch, Haddix tried to throw a slider down and away. But he got it a little too high, and it hung. Adcock pounced on it, slamming a drive deep to right center.

Bill Virdon and Joe Christopher raced back.

Virdon leaped at the wall, but luck had finally run out for the Pirates and Harvey Haddix. The ball sailed right over Virdon's glove 375 feet from home plate. Home run! Adcock hesitated, then ran to first. The crowd went wild.

The no-hitter was gone. The shutout was gone. The victory was gone.

The game was over. Harvey Haddix, after pitching the greatest game in baseball history, was the losing pitcher. He walked quickly to the Pittsburgh dugout.

What Happened Afterward

The excitement wasn't quite over. Mantilla crossed the plate with the game-winning run. But after rounding second base, Hank Aaron didn't see the ball clear the wall. He figured Adcock had just gotten a base hit to win the game. Aaron jubilantly trotted back to the dugout via the pitcher's mound without bothering to tag third base and home plate.

Adcock, naturally, completed his home-run trot, and most fans left the ballpark thinking the final score was 3–0. Milwaukee manager Fred Haney sent Aaron back out on the field to touch all the bases, but by that time Adcock had rounded third.

Umpire Frank Dascoli ruled that Adcock was out for passing Aaron on the bases. The final score was 2–0, not 3–0. (Actually, the score would change *again* the next day. Read on.)

◆ In the Pittsburgh clubhouse, Harvey Haddix showed a lot of class. After all he'd been through, he could have hidden in the trainer's room or beat a hasty retreat out of the stadium. Instead, he sat at his locker as reporters gathered around and calmly said, "Gentlemen, what can I do for you?"

The questions came fast and furious.

"Were you nervous?"

"I was more tired than nervous."

"Do you realize you've made baseball history?"

"All I know is that we lost. What's so historic about that? Didn't anyone else ever lose a 13-inning shutout?"

"What were you thinking about in the thirteenth inning?"

"All I kept thinking of was trying to keep them from scoring."

"Were you aware you were pitching a perfect game?"

"I knew I had a no-hitter—knew it all the time. I didn't know I had a perfect game. I thought I might have walked a man somewhere along the line."

"What about the pitch that Adcock hit over the wall?"

"It was a bad pitch. I made a few other mistakes, but I got away with them. I guess I should have walked Adcock."

"When did you start to tire?"

"During the last two innings."

"How do you feel?"

"It's just another loss—and they're not good."

♦ The Pirates felt terrible that they hadn't been able to score a single run for Haddix. Don Hoak in particular considered himself responsible because of the throwing error he made in the thirteenth inning. He apologized to Haddix, but the pitcher never blamed anyone. He knew his teammates had given it their best.

♦ Lew Burdette joked that an experienced pitcher like Harvey Haddix should have known better than to "bunch his hits."

"We got another mark there in the left-hand [win] column," Burdette said. "That's all that matters." But he added, "He deserved to win."

♦ Harvey Haddix didn't go to bed that night. He walked the streets of Milwaukee until morning, thinking, most likely, how unfair life can be sometimes.

♦ Haddix was invited to appear on *The Ed Sullivan Show* and *What's My Line*, but turned down both offers.

♦ The next day National League president Warren Giles ruled that Adcock's hit was a double, because Adcock had passed Aaron on the baselines. Only Mantilla's run counted, and the final score of the game was 1–0. Adcock lost what would have been his fourth homer of the year (he would go on to hit 25), and two RBIs.

♦ On his next start, Harvey Haddix was greeted with a

standing ovation in Pittsburgh. He didn't pitch a perfect game or a no-hitter this time, but he got a win. He gave up eight hits, throwing a 3–0 shutout.

Before the game, Warren Giles presented him with a silver tray and a dozen sterling goblets. The tray was inscribed: "To Harvey Haddix—in recognition of his outstanding performance—unprecedented in baseball history—pitching 12 consecutive perfect innings—game of May 26, 1959."

♦ Pittsburgh faded and finished the season in fourth place. Milwaukee finished in a tie with the Los Angeles Dodgers, and the Dodgers won both games of a playoff to determine the National League pennant. They won the World Series, too.

♦ During the off-season, Lew Burdette claimed he was the greatest pitcher who ever lived, and asked for a $10,000 raise. "The greatest game that was ever pitched in baseball wasn't good enough to beat me," explained Burdette, "so I've *got* to be the greatest."

The next season *Burdette* pitched a no-hitter, beating the Phillies 1–0.

♦ Harvey Haddix pitched six more years, never winning more than 11 games in a season. His lifetime record was 136–113 with an ERA of 3.63. For decades after his historic game, he would receive four or five letters a week from fans who remembered it.

♦ As of this writing, there have been seven perfect games *since* the Haddix masterpiece. Catfish Hunter pitched one in 1968, Jim Bunning in 1964, Sandy Koufax in 1965, Len

Barker in 1981, Mike Witt in 1984, Tom Browning in 1988, and Dennis Martinez in 1991.

♦ Haddix lost his no-hitter and perfect game for a *second* time 32 years later, when baseball commissioner Fay Vincent ruled that no-hitters were defined as games of nine innings or more that end with a team getting no hits. Since Haddix *did* give up a hit in the game, it is not *officially* a no-hitter.

But the Haddix game is the most famous no-hitter in baseball history, even if it wasn't a no-hitter. It will be remembered long after the *real* no-hitters have been forgotten.

For Baseball Trivia Lovers . . .

♦ Several other pitchers have lost no-hitters in extra innings: Bobo Newsom (1934), Tom Hughes (1910), Leon Ames (1909), Harry McIntire (1906), and Earl Moore (1901).

One day in 1917, Fred Toney of the Reds and Jim Vaughn of the Cubs each threw a no-hitter *against* the other. Toney won when the Reds pushed across a run in the tenth inning.

♦ One pitcher threw an official no-hitter even though he gave up a *hit*. In 1923, Howard Ehmke of the Red Sox was in the middle of a no-hitter when Slim Harris hit a double. But Harris forgot to touch first base. The hit was disallowed and Ehmke completed his no-hitter.

♦ Harvey Haddix got his first major-league victory against the Braves in 1952 when they were the Boston Braves. The losing pitcher—Lew Burdette.

♦ Eddie Mathews played with the Braves when they were in Boston, Milwaukee, and Atlanta, making him the only three-city player with a single franchise.

♦ Hall of Famers who played in this game: Aaron and Mathews.

♦ The very next season, many of these same Pittsburgh Pirates were involved in *another* one of the greatest games ever played. To read about that one, turn the page.

CHAPTER
4
The
Mazeroski Game

THE DATE: Thursday, October 13, 1960.
THE PLACE: Forbes Field,
Pittsburgh.
THE SITUATION: Game 7 of the World Series
between the New York Yankees
and Pittsburgh Pirates.

Yogi Berra (George Brace)

Bill Mazeroski (NBL)

NS GO WILD

ed for Collapse in 1959,
eroski Becomes Bucs 'Hero

right 'pennant
second in 1958,
Last year's
hopes didn't m
in serious
Pirates, a stror
were a disappo
In such a sit
porters of the t

Mazeroski heads jubilantly home. It was the first time the
World Series ever ended with a home run. (AP/Wide World Photos)

$\mathcal{S}$TATISTICS DON'T ALWAYS TELL the whole story. Take a look at these numbers and guess which team won the 1960 World Series.

	Yankees	Pirates
Runs scored	55	27
Hits	91	60
Batting average	.338	.256
Home runs	10	4
Extra base hits	27	15
Earned run average	3.54	7.11

It was blowout, right?

Now add the fact that the Yankees won the World Series six times in the 1950s, while the Pirates came in *last place* six times.

Also, during the regular season, the Yankees juggernaut led by Mickey Mantle and Roger Maris pounded out 193 home runs to set an American League record. The Pirates didn't have a single player who hit 25 home runs or had 100 RBIs.

Finally, during the World Series, the Yanks clobbered the Pirates in three games by the scores of 16–3, 10–0, and 12–0. That's a combined score of 38–3.

But thanks to their spectacular fielding, timely hitting and a stubborn refusal to give up, the underdog Pirates managed to win games 1, 4, and 5. The World Series came

down to one final showdown—a game that would turn
around on a bad-hop grounder.

It just goes to show that sometimes luck can be as important as statistics.

FIRST INNING. It was a warm and sunny day in Pittsburgh. The town, which hadn't won a World Series in 35
years, was going baseball crazy. Somebody hung a 40-foot
banner downtown that read STOP YANKEE AGGRESSION! A
murder trial had been postponed because it was believed
the jury wouldn't be able to concentrate on the evidence
during the World Series.

Vernon Law, who had already won Games 1 and 4, was
the starting pitcher for the Pirates. He was a control pitcher,
and his 20–9 record had earned him the Cy Young award.
Law retired the Yankees in the first inning.

FOR THE YANKS the starting pitcher was Bullet Bob Turley. Two years earlier, *he* had been the Cy Young winner,
but this season he only won nine games. Turley could throw
a baseball in the 90 mph range, despite an unusual "no-
windup" delivery.

Bob Turley didn't know he would be pitching this game
until he opened his locker and found a baseball in one of
his shoes. That was Yankees manager Casey Stengel's signal
to a pitcher that he would be the starter of the day.

Before game time, Casey gathered the Yankees around
him and told them, "Win or lose, it's been a good year, and

I want to thank you for everything." The words meant more than he let on at the time.

In the first inning, Turley got Pittsburgh center fielder Bill Virdon to fly out to left and shortstop Dick Groat to pop out to short. Bob Skinner, the left fielder, walked. Two outs, runner on first.

The batter was left-handed Rocky Nelson, a journeyman first baseman who'd played for six teams in 16 years. Nelson had a weird batting stance—both of his feet faced the pitcher. But his real claim to fame was that he would chew a wad of tobacco for an hour without spitting.

Turley ran the count to two balls and one strike on Nelson. The next pitch was about eye high and outside, but Rocky swung anyway and managed to pull a drive to right field. The ball looked like a sure double, but it kept carrying and just cleared the 30-foot screen 350 feet from the plate.

Two-run homer! Pirates 2, Yankees 0. Nelson's shot was the first Pittsburgh home run since Game 1.

The next batter was Roberto Clemente, who had yet to blossom into the Hall of Fame star he would later become. Turley got Clemente on a pop up to second to end the inning.

The Yankees bullpen was already warming up. When you're playing the seventh game of the World Series, there's no tomorrow.

SECOND INNING. Again Vernon Law retired the Yankees easily, and again the Pirates came to the plate swinging. Smoky Burgess, the big, slow-footed catcher, started the attack when he rammed a single down the right-field line. That was all it took for Yankees manager Casey Stengel to come out to the mound.

Bob Turley, having thrown just 20 pitches, was finished for the day. In came 22-year-old rookie Bill Stafford, who had pitched five scoreless innings in Game 5.

Runner on first, nobody out. Stafford couldn't seem to find the plate, and he walked third baseman Don Hoak on four pitches. Next up was Pittsburgh second baseman Bill Mazeroski.

The crew-cutted Maz was playing the World Series with his father Lew in mind. Years earlier, Lew Mazeroski was about to go for a tryout with the Cleveland Indians when he lost part of his foot in a coal mining accident. It ruined his baseball career. He lived to see his son Bill play in the majors, but not in the World Series. He had died of cancer a year earlier.

Mazeroski dropped a perfect bunt down the third-base line. Stafford grabbed the rolling ball and tried to make the play at first, but his throw was late. Now the bases were loaded, with nobody out.

Casey Stengel came out of the Yankees dugout for a chat with Stafford, and decided to leave him in the game. Vernon Law, the Pirates pitcher, was up, and a ground ball would make an easy double play for the Yankees.

That's exactly what happened. Law bounced a one-hopper back to the mound. Stafford speared it and threw home to get one out. Yankees catcher Johnny Blanchard, filling in for the injured Elston Howard, whipped the ball to first to complete the double play.

It looked like Stafford was going to get the Yankees out of the jam when he got two strikes on Bill Virdon, but on the next pitch Virdon lashed a broken-bat single to right. Hoak and Mazeroski scored.

Dick Groat bounced to third to end the inning, but the Pirates now had a commanding 4–0 lead.

Four runs should stand up to beat just about any team in baseball. But you have to take into consideration that the Pirates were playing the New York Yankees. The *Mickey Mantle / Roger Maris / Yogi Berra / Whitey Ford* New York Yankees.

THIRD AND FOURTH INNINGS. There was no scoring in the third or fourth inning.

The Yankees brought in left-hander Bobby Shantz. One of the smallest men in baseball at five foot six and 139 pounds, Shantz was a Gold Glove winner and the American League's Most Valuable Player in 1952, when he went 24–7.

FIFTH INNING. Vernon Law had been holding the mighty Yanks scoreless on just two hits, but it was nearly impossible to keep the Bronx Bombers down for long.

The first batter in the fifth inning was Moose Skowron, who was the only Yankee to hit .300 for the season (.309). Skowron was a big man, but that's not why he was nicknamed Moose. When he was a baby, Bill Skowron's grand-father called him Mussolini (presumably because the infant resembled the Italian dictator). The rest of the family short-ened it to Moose.

Skowron had 26 home runs for the season, and he had hit one in Game 4. Law was pitching carefully to him, but Moose blasted an outside pitch into the right-field stands just inside the foul line. Pirates 4, Yankees 1.

Law retired the next three New Yorkers without further damage.

SIXTH INNING. Second baseman Bobby Richardson led off the sixth for the Yankees. Richardson, who hit just one home run all year with 26 RBIs, had socked a grand slam in Game 3 and was having a spectacular Series. This time up he lined a single into short center-field.

Tony Kubek, the Yankees shortstop, walked on a full count to put runners at first and second.

It looked like Vernon Law had had enough. Pirates man-ager Danny Murtaugh came out to the mound, patted Law on the shoulder, and took the baseball from his hand. Law walked off the field to a standing ovation from the grateful Pirates fans.

Out of the Pittsburgh bullpen marched Elroy Leon Face, the best relief pitcher in baseball. The previous year, Face had an astounding 18–1 record, and he had won 22 straight games over two seasons. At one stretch, Face appeared in 93 games without a loss.

Elroy Face had been a fastball pitcher, and in 1954 he was sent down to the minors to learn to throw a change-up. Instead, he taught himself the forkball, which is called a split-finger fastball today. He rode the pitch back to the big leagues, and it made him a star.

Pittsburgh's usual strategy was simple—get a lead and bring in Face. He had already saved Games 1, 4, and 5 for the Pirates.

Okay, where were we? Bottom of the sixth, Yankee runners on first and second, with nobody out. Face got the always dangerous Roger Maris to foul out to third, but Mickey Mantle knocked a ground single past the diving Groat into center field. Bobby Richardson scored, and it was Pirates 4, Yankees 2. Tony Kubek was on third base, and the game was getting interesting.

Next up was Yogi Berra. The Hall of Fame Yankees catcher had been the American League MVP in 1951, 1954, and 1955, but he was 35 years old now and playing left field to rest his legs.

The count went full, and Face threw Yogi a slider down and in. The squat Berra, known for swinging at just about anything, walloped the ball all the way into the upper deck of Forbes Field. It landed just inside the right-field foul line for a three-run home run. It was Yogi's eleventh World Series round tripper. Now the *Yankees* were in the driver's seat, 5–4.

Carlton Fisk (see Chapter 2) is famous for the body English he put on the ball when he waved his famous home run fair in the 1975 World Series. But actually, Yogi Berra pioneered the art. Here's how *The Philadelphia Inquirer* described his home run:

"As the ball sailed up into the air, Yogi hopped his way down to first, giving it body English in an attempt to wish it fair, and when it plopped into the upper deck, fair by inches, Yogi leaped high into the air at first base and jubilantly jigged his way home behind Kubek and Mantle."

EIGHTH INNING. Elroy Face was still pitching for Pittsburgh, and he got past the Yankees' two toughest hitters, Roger Maris and Mickey Mantle. Two outs.

That brought up Yogi Berra. Having given up a home run to Yogi the last time up, Face wasn't taking any chances. He walked him. Moose Skowron bounced an infield single into the hole at short, putting runners at first and second with two outs.

Johnny Blanchard ripped a single to right center, scoring Berra. Yankees 6, Pirates 4. Next, Yankees third baseman Clete Boyer doubled down the left-field line and Skowron scored. Yankees 7, Pirates 4.

With just six more outs remaining for Pittsburgh, it looked like the World Series was just about over. The Yankees were unbeatable.

BUT DURING THE REGULAR SEASON, the Pirates had won 23 games in their final turn at bat, and they weren't about to give up. In the bottom of the eighth, Gino Cimoli pinch-hit for Elroy Face and bumped a single into right field off Bobby Shantz. Shantz had pitched five scoreless innings at this point.

The next play turned the game around. Bill Virdon was the hitter. On an 0–1 pitch from Shantz, Virdon slapped a hard grounder straight at shortstop Tony Kubek. As they say in baseball lingo, it had double play written all over it.

But Forbes Field was known for its rock-hard infield. The ball hit a tiny rut in the dirt and took a crazy hop over Kubek's glove. It was probably the most famous bad hop in baseball history.

"The ball was going to hit me between the eyes or in the nose," Kubek said later, "but I threw my head back."

It struck the shortstop right in his throat. Tony fell backward and to his right. The ball bounced toward second base and both runners were safe. Kubek was on the ground, clutching his neck and choking. His uniform was soaked with blood.

"Give him room!" shouted Casey Stengel as the Yankees gathered around. "Give him room!"

Kubek kept trying to tell Casey he wanted to stay in the game, but no words came out. After some struggling, he got to his feet and was helped off the field. He was rushed to Pittsburgh Eye and Ear Hospital. The doctors forbade him to speak, but allowed him to respond to a yes/no question with a head shake.

"Would Virdon's grounder have been a double play if not

for the crazy hop?" Kubek was asked. The young shortstop nodded his head yes.

BACK AT THE BALLPARK, Joe DeMaestri came out to replace Kubek at shortstop. Because of the freak play, instead of two outs and nobody on, the Pirates had two on and nobody out. The tying run was at bat, Dick Groat.

All Groat had done during the regular season was lead the National League in hitting (.325) and win the Most Valuable Player award. He lined a single past third base, scoring Cimoli and sending Virdon to second. Yankees 7, Pirates 5.

Stengel came out to the mound once again. That would be all for Bobby Shantz. (And it would be all for Casey, too. Few knew it at the time, but this would be the Ol' Perfessor's last appearance on the field in a Yankees uniform.) Jim Coates came in to pitch.

Bob Skinner bunted to advance the runners to second and third. That put the tying run in scoring position. Rocky Nelson stepped up and hit a fly ball to right field, but it wasn't deep enough for the runners to tag up.

The next batter was Roberto Clemente. He swung wildly at a few bad pitches, then squibbed a little dribbler down the first-base line. Skowron was playing deep and came in to pick up the grounder.

Jim Coates, the Yankees pitcher, should have dashed over to cover first base, but he didn't move off the pitcher's mound. Skowron and Clemente had a footrace to the bag and the speedy Pirate won it. Clemente was safe on first, Groat on third, and Virdon scored.

Yankees 7, Pirates 6. The Pirates were not dead yet.

The next hitter was Hal Smith, a bench-warming catcher who had been brought in to run for Smoky Burgess. Smith was a former Yankees minor leaguer, which gave him an added motivation to hit against his old team.

He gave them something to think about by slamming a 2–2 fastball over the ivy-covered brick wall in left field. Yogi Berra didn't bother to chase it. It was gone with the crack of the bat. Coates flung his glove in the air in disgust.

A five-run inning! The Pirates had been down 7–4, and now they were ahead 9–7.

Sports Illustrated wrote that Dick Groat "danced hilariously across the plate" and Clemente "came leaping down the line like a kangaroo." Smith, of course, had a huge grin on his face as he touched the plate. The crowd in Forbes Field was going crazy. Coming into the final inning, they could smell the world championship.

Hal Smith's home run would have been one of the most famous in baseball history, and this chapter would have been called "The Smith Game." But the game wasn't over yet.

NINTH INNING. With just three outs separating the Pirates from the World Championship, Pittsburgh play-by-

play announcer Bob Prince made his way down to the clubhouse to interview the victorious Bucs. Eighteen-game winner Bob Friend was brought in to nail down the last three
outs for the Pirates.

But the Yanks were not being cooperative. Bobby Richardson greeted Friend with a single to left, his eleventh hit
of the World Series. Former Pirate Dale Long, pinch-hitting
for DeMaestri, singled to right. Richardson stopped at second base.

Suddenly, the Yankees had the tying run on base and the
winning run at the plate in the name of a guy who could
hit a little—Roger Maris. Maris was the American League's
Most Valuable Player, with 39 home runs and a league-
leading 112 runs batted in.

Bob Friend had only thrown five pitches, but Danny Murtaugh didn't want to see a sixth. He yanked Friend and
brought in left-hander Harvey Haddix, who had been the
winner of Game 5. The previous May, Haddix achieved baseball immortality by pitching a perfect game through 12
innings and then losing the game in the thirteenth (see
Chapter 3).

Haddix got Maris to foul out behind the plate, freezing
the runners. But the next hitter, Mickey Mantle, drove the
second pitch up the middle for a single. Richardson scored,
making it Pirates 9, Yanks 8. Dale Long took third base on
the hit. Gil McDougald was brought in to pinch-run for
Long.

SO HERE WE ARE: top of the ninth inning, a one-run ball-game with runners on first and third. One out. The Pirates could end the thing right now with a ground ball.

The batter was Yogi Berra, who hit the three-run homer earlier in the game. This time, he hit a ground ball toward first. Yogi Berra was not a fast runner. All first baseman Rocky Nelson had to do was pick up the ball, throw to second for the force play on Mickey Mantle, and catch the return throw for a World Series–ending double play.

Instead, Nelson tried to make the double play the *hard* way. He picked up the bouncing ball and stepped on first base. That was the second out of the inning.

But at this moment Mickey Mantle, who was never known as a baseball genius, made the heads-up play of his life. He realized that as soon as Nelson tagged first, there was no longer a force play at second base. So instead of running there into a sure out, Mantle hovered near the first base bag.

Nelson had his arm cocked, ready to throw to second when he realized Mantle was next to him. Nelson dove for Mantle. Mantle dove for the bag.

Safe!

Had Nelson made the tag, the Series would have been over. Instead, Gil McDougald raced home from third base with the tying run. Pirates 9, Yankees 9.

Mickey Mantle had saved the game for the Yankees. Not by slamming a tremendous home run, or making a great catch, but by using his head.

WHAT AN INCREDIBLE SEESAW BATTLE! First Pittsburgh had a four-run lead, then the Yankees battled back to tie it. Then the Yankees took a three-run lead and Pittsburgh tied it. Then Pittsburgh took a two-run lead and the Yankees tied it.

It was an emotionally draining game for everyone in the stadium and millions of fans around the country.

The Yankees couldn't score a go-ahead run. Moose Skowron bounced to Dick Groat at shortstop. Groat flipped the ball to Mazeroski for the force play that ended the inning.

As Bill Mazeroski jogged back to the dugout and tossed the ball on the mound, little did he realize that he and that baseball were about to make history.

PITTSBURGH BROADCASTER BOB PRINCE, remember, had gone down to the Pirates clubhouse after the eighth inning to congratulate the winners. When the Yankees tied the game up in the ninth, he hustled out of there and made his way back toward the broadcast booth. He didn't want to be in the Pirates locker room if the Yankees were going to win the Series.

Before the Yankees charged out on the field in the bottom of the ninth, Casey Stengel gathered his team around him and barked, "All right! Let's get these National League phonies!"

The Yanks now had their fifth pitcher of the game on the mound, 25-year-old Ralph Terry. Terry had come in to get the final out in the eighth inning. He had pitched six innings in Game 4, and was the loser.

A tall, hard-throwing right-hander, Terry had a blazing fastball but insisted on experimenting with breaking pitches.

Up to the plate stepped 23-year-old Bill Mazeroski. Maz wasn't known as a hitter. He was a glove man and perhaps the best defensive player in the game.

Some of the Pirates called him No-Touch because he got rid of the ball so quickly during double plays, it seemed like he hadn't even touched it. Others called him Tree Stump for the way he stayed right at the bag when runners were bearing down on him. Mazeroski would win eight Gold Glove awards during his career.

But he could hit when he had to. He'd socked 11 home runs on the season, and probably would have hit a lot more if he didn't play his home games in cavernous Forbes Field. Maz hit a homer in Game 1 that turned out to be the margin of victory.

The previous season, Mazeroski received much of the blame for the Pirates' fourth-place finish, when he gained some weight and slowed down in the field and at bat. His father's passing away probably had something to do with his disappointing season.

As he stepped to the plate in the bottom of the ninth, Maz was surely thinking that if the Pirates could push across just one run, they would be champions of the world.

The Pirates pitchers Vernon Law and Elroy Face were in

the clubhouse now, listening to the game on the radio. The Forbes Field crowd was screaming for a Pirates hit.

Yankees scouting reports said the way to get Mazeroski out was to throw low curveballs. Ralph Terry kicked his leg high and went into his windup. Mazeroski let the first pitch, a high slider, go by for ball one.

Yankees catcher Johnny Blanchard marched out to the mound. "Keep the ball down!" he warned Terry. The clock at the top of the scoreboard in left field said 3:35 P.M.

Bob Prince was still making his way back to the broadcast booth when Terry threw his second pitch. It was high, it was a fastball, and Mazeroski took a vicious swing at it. The ball leaped off the bat on a flight path toward left field.

Mazeroski was running hard to first. He didn't see the ball. Yogi Berra took a few steps back, then stopped. It was a dry fall day, and the ball was carrying well.

It was deep, deep, and . . . gone! The ball sailed over the scoreboard and landed in the trees. Pittsburgh 10, Yankees 9! There would be no more comebacks today. The Pirates, who were known for pitching and defense, had beaten the Yankees at their own game. They won their first World Series in 35 years with a home run—the only time in baseball history that the Series ended with a four-bagger.

As he was heading for second base, Mazeroski heard screaming and saw the umpire down the left-field line waving his arms in a circle to indicate home run.

Maz pulled off his cap and swung it around his head

jubilantly. Fans were all over the field by then, so he had to fight his way around the bases past a dozen or so back-slapping Pirates rooters. Umpire Bill Jackowski did his best to clear a path for Maz to touch home plate.

It was pandemonium in Pittsburgh. Confetti began falling from office buildings until it was ankle deep. Three hundred thousand people gathered downtown to snake-dance through the streets. Radio and TV stations urged people to stay away from the city. Two tunnels were closed to traffic.

The fans nearly tore down Forbes Field. Somebody ran onto the field with a shovel, dug up home plate, and made off with it.

Bob Prince was still on his way to the press box when he heard the roar of the crowd. He never saw Mazeroski's home run.

A 14-year-old boy named Andy Jerpe picked up the bouncing baseball outside Forbes Field. He brought it to the Pittsburgh clubhouse to present it to Bill Mazeroski. Maz signed his name on the ball and handed it back to Andy Jerpe.

"You keep it, son," he said. "The memory is good enough for me."

What Happened Afterward

The Yankees locker room was like a morgue, except for an occasional "I can't believe it" from the ballplayers. Mickey Mantle sobbed uncontrollably in the trainer's room.

"A cold chill ran down my back a moment after I hit that

ball," said Bill Mazeroski after the game. "For a second there, I didn't know quite what to do. But the message finally got to my legs, and I set sail. I can't begin to describe how I felt when I saw the ball clear the fence. Time seemed to stand still for an instant."

Ralph Terry wasn't as eloquent when he was asked what pitch he had thrown to Mazeroski. "I don't know what the pitch was," he grumbled. "All I know is, it was the wrong one."

In private, Terry walked over to his manager and said, "Casey, I hate to have it end this way."

"What were you trying to throw him?" Stengel asked the heartbroken pitcher. Terry replied that he was trying to keep the ball low.

"As long as you were trying to pitch him the right way, I'm going to sleep easy at night," Stengel replied.

◆ A few hours after Mazeroski hit his home run, John F. Kennedy and Richard Nixon engaged in the third debate of their presidential campaigns.

◆ Tony Kubek was able to speak the next day, but in a whisper. Ironically, the one man in baseball history to have his voice knocked out by a batted ball would later become a popular TV broadcaster.

In his book *Sixty-One*, Kubek wrote, "For nine years I played in the majors, but I'm known as the guy who got hit in the throat."

◆ The Yankees, to a man, believed the Pirates had won despite the fact that they were an inferior team. "In all my

World Series experience," Mickey Mantle wrote in his autobiography *The Mick*, "that was the one time when I really thought the better team had lost."

But Pirates manager Danny Murtaugh put it into perspective: "You don't win the Series on total runs. You win it on the most runs in the final game. We'll just take the one Mazeroski hit, and they can have the rest."

♦ Four days after the World Series, Casey Stengel was fired, mostly because the Yankees' management believed he was too old. "I'll never make the mistake of being seventy again," Casey quipped. In 12 seasons with the Yanks, Stengel had won ten pennants and seven World Championships.

He received a lot of criticism for starting Art Ditmar in Game 1 instead of his ace, Whitey Ford. Ditmar ended up losing Game 1 (he didn't even make it through the first inning) and Game 5, while Ford pitched complete game shutouts in Game 3 and Game 6. If Ford had started the opening game, he would have been able to pitch three games of the Series instead of two.

"I loved Casey," Mickey Mantle said later, "but I really believe that Casey blew the 1960 World Series." In an interview 12 years later, Casey admitted he'd made a mistake in starting Ditmar instead of Ford.

Casey went on to manage the newborn New York Mets for their first four seasons. They came in last each year. He died in 1975, at age 85.

♦ The season after Mazeroski's blast, Roger Maris of the Yankees hit 61 home runs, breaking Babe Ruth's "unbreakable" record. The Yankees won the World Series this time, and the Pirates fell to fourth place.

♦ Ralph Terry's career would soar after he gave up one of the most famous home runs in World Series history. He would post a 16–3 record the next season and a 23–12 mark in 1962.

Once again he was on the mound for the final pitch of the 1962 World Series, but this time he was the winner after throwing a four-hit shutout. Terry was named the World Series Most Valuable Player that year.

For Baseball Trivia Lovers . . .

♦ In this World Series, 65 records were set and 27 were tied. Yogi Berra alone set 14 records (partly because he played two positions). Though the Yankees set nearly all the records, it was the Bucs who had the crown.

♦ The two World Series' heroes, Bill Mazeroski and Bobby Richardson, both hit in the number eight position in the lineup. Richardson was named Most Valuable Player of the Series, the first time the award went to a member of the losing team.

♦ The winning pitcher of the Mazeroski Game was . . . who else? Harvey Haddix. It was his second win of the Series.

♦ I can't resist telling you that the Pirates had a pitcher named Vinegar Bend Mizell. He pitched two and one-third innings in Game 3, giving up four runs. Vinegar Bend was the losing pitcher, and his earned run average was 15.43.

♦ Yankees third baseman Clete Boyer had two brothers

who played in the majors—Ken and Cloyd. (Cloyd!) In the seventh game of the 1964 World Series, Clete and Ken (of the Cardinals) made history when both Boyer brothers hit home runs.

♦ Forbes Field was named after a British general of the French and Indian War. In 61 years, not a single no-hitter was pitched there. Babe Ruth hit the final three homers of his career in Forbes on May 25, 1935. The last one, number 714, was the first home run to clear the roof of the right-field stands.

Forbes was torn down in 1970, when Three Rivers Stadium was completed. Today, the University of Pittsburgh library is located where Forbes Field stood.

♦ The Yankees and Pirates also opposed each other in the 1927 World Series. The Yanks, with their "Murderer's Row" lineup of Babe Ruth, Lou Gehrig, Tony Lazzeri, Bob Meusel, and Earle Combs, demolished Pittsburgh in four straight games.

♦ One other World Series is famous for a bad hop. In 1924, the Washington Senators defeated the New York Giants in the seventh game when a grounder hit a pebble and leaped over third baseman Fred Lindstrom's head.

♦ Dale Long was the first left-handed catcher in the major leagues. In May of 1956, he set a record when he hit eight home runs in eight consecutive games. The mark was tied 32 years later by Don Mattingly of the Yankees, and again in 1993 by Ken Griffey, Jr.

♦ Pirates third baseman Don Hoak was involved in a bizarre incident on April 21, 1957, when he was playing for the Cincinnati Reds. He was the runner at second, and there was another Red on first. A ground ball was hit toward the shortstop, and Hoak, maybe out of habit, fielded the ball and flipped it to the baffled shortstop.

After that, a rule was instituted making the runner and batter out if the runner interfered with a batted ball.

♦ Looking at pictures of Casey Stengel, it seems like he was always an old man, but Casey had a solid big-league career as a player before he started managing. He went 4 for 4 in his first game for the Brooklyn Dodgers back in 1912. He hit .364 in the 1916 World Series and hit two game-winning home runs in the 1923 World Series. Over 14 seasons, he hit .284 with 131 stolen bases and 60 home runs.

His real name, by the way, was Charles Stengel. He was called Casey in honor of his hometown, Kansas City.

♦ Bill Mazeroski was brought up in a tiny Ohio town named Witch Hazel. These other famous athletes were raised within about four miles of there: Phil and Joe Niekro, basketball star John Havlicek, football Hall of Famers Clarke Hinkle and Lou Groza, as well as Notre Dame coach Lou Holtz.

♦ Singer Bing Crosby was a part owner of the Pittsburgh Pirates.

♦ Vernon Law and his wife VaNita had six children. They named them Veldon, Veryl, Vaughn, Varlin, VaLynda, and Vance.

Like his dad, Vance Law played for the Pittsburgh Pirates—as well as four other teams in the 1980s.

CHAPTER
5

The $15,000 "Slide"

THE DATE: Saturday, October 23, 1886.
THE PLACE: Sportsman's Park, St. Louis.
THE SITUATION: The final game of the championship series between the Chicago White Stockings of the National League and the St. Louis Brown Stockings of the American Association.

Curt Welch (NBL)

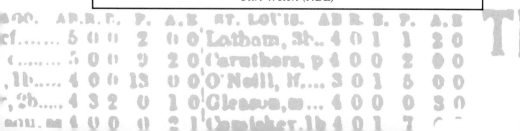

Arlie Latham 65 years after the greatest game of the 19th century. He was 91 years old, and the oldest living major league baseball player at the time. (AP/Wide World Photos)

*B*ASEBALL DIDN'T BEGIN the day Babe Ruth socked his first home run in 1915. The game had already been around for 75 years by that time.

And the World Series didn't begin in 1903, as most people believe. It began in 1882 when the Chicago White Stockings took on the Cincinnati Reds. The White Stockings were the winners of the National League pennant, and the Reds were tops in the American Association, a major league that lasted from 1881 to 1890.

A book of the greatest games in baseball history should include *at least* one from the game's first century, and the game between the White Stockings and St. Louis Browns that took place on October 23, 1886, is the most memorable of "the dead ball era."*

THE CHICAGO WHITE STOCKINGS were baseball's first dynasty. They won the first National League pennant in 1876, and also won in 1880, 1881, 1882, and 1885. In 1886 they came in first once again, with a 90–34 record. There were eight teams in each league in those days.

Chicago had it all—the best hitters, the best pitchers, and an infield known as "The Stone Wall."

The St. Louis Browns won the *other* pennant—the American Association pennant—in 1885 and 1886. St. Louis didn't have the muscle of the White Stockings, but they

---

*The baseballs were truly dead in those days. In fact, Hank Stovey led the league with just *seven* home runs in 1886. The "lively ball era" wouldn't begin until 1910, when cork centers were inserted into baseballs to make them travel farther.

used skillful baserunning, fielding, and pitching to finish the 1886 season with an impressive 93–46 record.

The World Series was not an annual event in the 1800s. Near the end of the '86 season, Browns owner Chris Von Der Ahe wrote this letter to the president of the Chicago White Stockings, Albert Spalding:

"The championship season is fast approaching an end, and it now seems reasonably sure that the Chicago White Stockings and St. Louis Brown Stockings will win the championship of their respective associations. I therefore take this opportunity of challenging your team, on behalf of the Browns, for a series of contests to be known as the World's Championship Series."

Spalding's response:

"We'll play you under only one condition. Winner take all! And by all, I mean every dime that comes through the gate."

The two men agreed to a best-of-seven championship, just like today's World Series.

"I GOT DE BEST TEAM IN BASEBALL," crowed Chris Von Der Ahe. "My poys can lick any team in de world. As for dose White Stockings, bah, we make 'em look silly!"

The team owners of the 1800s were just as colorful as the George Steinbrenners and Ted Turners of today. Von Der Ahe was a German immigrant who had made his fortune selling beer in America. He called himself Der Boss President, and had a statue of himself built and installed in Sportsman's Park.

He was a man who enjoyed his wealth. After each home game, Von Der Ahe would pile all the gate receipts in a wheelbarrow and personally roll them to the bank.

Chris Von Der Ahe was a true baseball innovator. Legend has it that he introduced hot dogs to ballparks and installed the first ladies' room in a ballpark. It is also said that he coined the term *baseball fan* when he referred to people attending games as "fanatics." Most people still called baseball lovers "kranks" in the 1880s.

THE PRESIDENT OF THE CHICAGO WHITE STOCKINGS was former pitcher Albert Spalding. In 1876 he and his brother invested $800 to start a sporting goods store in Chicago. The Spaldings became millionaires, and you're probably playing with some Spalding equipment today.

As a player, Al Spalding was baseball's first 200-game winner, and one season he won 57 games and lost just 5. His motto was, "Everything is possible to him who dares."

Spalding promised his players new suits and half the receipts if they won the championship series against the Browns.

The first three games took place in Chicago, where the White Stockings won two. The next three were in St. Louis. The Browns won the first two games to take a 3–2 lead in the series. Chicago needed to win Game 6 or it would be all over.

BASEBALL WAS A DIFFERENT GAME in 1886. There was no pitcher's mound, for one thing. Hurlers threw from a rectangular box 50 feet from home plate, and they could take a run and a jump before delivering the ball. A pitcher could throw seven pitches out of the strike zone before giving up a base on balls. He probably *needed* them. Overhand pitching had only been legalized a year earlier and many pitchers were still getting the hang of it.

A batter could request that the pitcher throw the ball high or low in the strike zone. If he walked, it was recorded as a hit. If he overran first base on a single, he could be tagged out. If he fouled a ball into the stands, the game would be stopped and everybody would go look for it. If a boy or girl returned the ball, the child was given a free admission.

Pinch hitting didn't exist. Substitutions were only made when a player was hurt, and hurt *badly*. Gloves were considered sissy, so most fielders didn't wear them.

Uniforms didn't have names or numbers on them. The top salary for a major-league ballplayer was $2,000 a year. Fans parked their cars and buggies in the outfield.

This is 1886, and the Civil War wasn't something people read about in history books. They *remembered* it. The telephone was just ten years old, and few people had one. There was no radio to listen to, and the Wright brothers wouldn't fly for another 17 years.

It was a different world, but just like today there were

three strikes, three outs, nine innings, and three bases 90 feet apart. They were playing the game of baseball, and the game they played on October 23 would be remembered as the greatest game in the 19th century.

I could not have written the play-by-play of this game without the October 24, 1886, edition of *The St. Louis Globe-Democrat*, which fortunately has been preserved on microfilm.

FIRST INNING. It was a dark and cloudy day in St. Louis. The threat of rain didn't prevent 11,500 fans from crowding into Sportsman's Park. There were only a few thousand bleacher seats, so the crowd overflowed the grandstand and stood in rows twelve deep in a circle outside the foul lines.

For the people who couldn't get in, *The St. Louis Globe-Democrat* set up bulletin boards outside their offices. Runs, hits, and errors were sent by telegraph from the ballpark to the newspaper, and the game was recreated on the board.

The Browns wore white uniforms with brown trim. The White Stockings were in royal blue with white caps and white silk socks.

"The Chicagos," as they were sometimes called, had a tradition of parading to the ballpark in an open, horse-drawn buggy. "We had 'em whipped before we even threw a ball," catcher Mike "King" Kelly used to say. "We had 'em scared to death."

Umpire Pierce tossed a coin to determine which team

would bat first—the custom in those days. St. Louis won the toss and elected to have "last licks." At precisely 2:18, Bob "Mighty Mite" Caruthers threw the first pitch of the game to George "Piano Legs" Gore.

Caruthers was just five foot seven and 138 pounds, but he could *pitch*. He won 40 games twice in his career (218–97), and had just come off a 30–6 season while batting .334. Caruthers had thrown a shutout in Game 2 of the Series.

George Gore was a perfect leadoff hitter for the White Stockings. He could hit for average (.360 in 1880), he led the National League in walks three times, and he once stole seven bases in a game. Gore got around on a pitch from Caruthers, but it went for a fly ball out to left field. One out.

Next up was Mike "King" Kelly, who led the league with a .388 average and 155 runs scored. Some histories of baseball say Kelly invented the hit-and-run play, and he popularized the hook slide. In fact, he was the inspiration for a hit song entitled "Slide Kelly Slide."

King Kelly was a tall, handsome man with a handlebar mustache and a thick shock of dark hair. He was baseball's first superstar personality. When he went out at night, he took along his Japanese valet and a monkey.

Kelly had an unusual batting stance. He stood with his back almost facing the catcher, holding his bat low. It didn't work this time. He popped the ball up weakly and Caruthers caught it on the fly. Two outs.

The third hitter in the Chicago lineup was another giant

of 19th-century baseball, Adrian "Cap" Anson. Anson hit .329 over a 22-year span, playing every game of his career for the White Stockings and managing the team for 19 years as well. This season Anson led the league in RBIs and came in second in batting average, hits, doubles, and slugging average. He hit the ball hard off Caruthers, but flied out to right field. Three outs.

"The outfielders were kept busy, and they did their work well," *The Globe-Democrat* wrote of the top of the first inning.

JOHN CLARKSON was the starting pitcher for Chicago. A year before, Clarkson had won an astonishing 53 games, including a no-hitter. He was 35–17 in 1886 and led the league in strikeouts. Clarkson was a fastballer, but he also had a "drop" pitch that hitters found baffling.

Old photos show him to be a thin man, with a waxed mustache and hair parted down the middle. A story is told that Clarkson once pitched a lemon instead of a baseball to prove to the umpire that it was too dark to play.

Clarkson struck out two of the three hitters he faced, and the Browns went down in order in the first inning. He had pitched a shutout in Game 1, and it looked like Clarkson was on top of his game again.

SECOND INNING. Chicago second baseman Fred Pfeffer started things off with a single to right. Pfeffer (.264) wasn't much with the bat, but he was one of the fastest players in the game and could circle the bases in less than 16 seconds. He promptly stole second base and advanced to third on a passed ball.

Runner on third, nobody out. It was a golden opportunity for the White Stockings to score early. But Bob Caruthers bore down and struck out Ned Williamson and Tommy Burns. Two outs.

The next hitter was rookie right fielder Jimmy Ryan. He singled to left and Fred Pfeffer trotted home from third base. Chicago 1, St. Louis 0.

THE BROWNS WENT DOWN 1, 2, 3 in their half of the second. St. Louis right fielder Dave Foutz, who was called Scissors because he was so skinny, almost got a hit on a fly ball to right.

"It looked to be safe," wrote *The Globe-Democrat*, "but Ryan made a run after it and caught it in fine style."

THIRD INNING. John Clarkson led off for the White Stockings. He popped the ball up in foul territory and Bob Caruthers dashed over to catch it. One out. George Gore hit an easy ground ball to third, but St. Louis third baseman Arlie Latham botched the throw to first. The ball got away and Gore went all the way around to third base. Runner on third, one out.

King Kelly was up. He also hit a grounder to third base. As Latham fielded the ball, he saw Gore trying to score from third. This time Latham's throw was true and Gore was out at the plate. That killed the possible rally for Chicago.

Once again, John Clarkson retired the Browns easily in the bottom half of the inning.

FOURTH AND FIFTH INNINGS. Sportsman's Park was just 285 feet down the right-field line. Fred Pfeffer led off for Chicago, and he slammed a fly ball to right that carried into the stands. Under 1886 rules, the ball was still in play. Right fielder Dave Foutz frantically climbed through the fans looking for it, but by the time he picked it up Pfeffer had circled the bases for a home run. Chicago 2, St. Louis 0.

Caruthers retired the rest of the White Stockings without giving up another run.

For the fourth time, John Clarkson retired the Browns in order.

Both teams went down 1, 2, 3 in the fifth.

SIXTH INNING. Fred Pfeffer, who always seemed to be in the middle of things, led off the sixth inning for the White Stockings. He slapped an easy grounder to Yank Robinson at second. Robinson was ambidextrous and didn't wear a glove, so he could pick up grounders and throw to any base with either hand. That talent didn't do him much good here, unfortunately—the ball went right through his legs.

Right fielder Dave Foutz backed up the play, but the ball

went through *his* legs, too. No wonder baseball players took to wearing gloves in the 1890s.

When the Browns finally got hold of the ball, Fred Pfeffer was standing on third base.

Ned Williamson stepped up to the plate. Williamson (.216) wasn't known for getting a lot of hits, but he could hit the ball *far.* He 27 home runs in 1884, an amazing total for the dead ball era. The record lasted 35 years, until a kid named Babe Ruth broke it.

Williamson didn't hit a home run this time, but he smacked a fly ball to deep right field. Fred Pfeffer tagged up and ran home after the catch. Now the White Stockings had a 3–0 lead. Fred Pfeffer had driven in one run and scored Chicago's two other runs.

Meanwhile, John Clarkson was working on a no-hitter for Chicago. Once again he set the Browns down in order.

SEVENTH INNING. Bob Caruthers seemed to be getting stronger as the game went on. He retired the White Stockings in order in the top of the seventh.

With one out for St. Louis, James "Tip" O'Neill came to bat. O'Neill had hit two home runs in Game 2. He was known for using one of the smallest bats in baseball, and he liked to purposely foul off pitch after pitch until the disgusted pitcher would walk him. That's why he was called Tip.

This time O'Neill hit the ball far and deep for the first St.

Louis hit. As the Chicago defense scrambled to throw the ball in, O'Neill tore around the bases. When he got to third he decided to stop, but his momentum carried him past the base. By that time Chicago third baseman Tommy Burns had the ball. He put the tag on O'Neill, and the hit was wasted.

At the end of seven innings, it was still Chicago 3, St. Louis 0. Despite the score, St. Louis fans could sense the tables were turning.

EIGHTH INNING. Once again, Bob Caruthers retired the White Stockings in order.

Leading off for St. Louis, first baseman Charlie Comiskey slapped a single to right. Runner on first, nobody out.

That brought up Curt Welch, one of the best center fielders of his day but not a great hitter. He tapped a slow grounder to third. Tommy Burns picked it cleanly, but threw the ball in the dirt at first, and Cap Anson couldn't come up with the short hop.

Dave Foutz, the Browns right fielder, was up. Foutz had a sparkling 41–16 record as a pitcher in 1886, but he played the field on days when he wasn't pitching.

Clarkson was starting to get rattled. He hadn't had to bother with base runners all day, and now there were men on first and second with no outs. He threw a low pitch to Foutz and it got past King Kelly for a passed ball. The runners advanced to second and third.

Foutz hit a fly ball to center field. After the catch, Charlie

Comiskey tagged up and crossed the plate. Finally, the Browns were on the scoreboard. Chicago 3, St. Louis 1.

Curt Welch advanced to third on the play. Runner on third, one out. Yank Robinson popped out weakly to first base for the second out, so Welch had to stay at third.

Doc Bushong, the Browns catcher, was up. He was called Doc because he studied dentistry in the off-season. Bushong walked, putting runners at first and third with two outs. The tying run was on base.

That brought up Arlie Latham, one of early baseball's real characters. Latham had the unusual nickname, the Freshest Man in the World. He was known more for his heckling and clowning than his skill with a bat. When he wasn't hitting, Latham would coach third base and run up and down the foul line taunting opposing players. These antics, some historians say, led to the coaches boxes we see next to first base and third base today.

The St. Louis crowd was getting revved up for the first time all afternoon. Clarkson worked the count to three balls and two strikes (remember, that wasn't a full count because pitchers could throw seven balls in those days). Latham stepped out of the batter's box and turned to the crowd.

"Don't get nervous, folks," he hollered. "I'll tie it up."

True to his word, on the next pitch Latham lashed the ball deep down the left-field line. Chicago left fielder Abner Dalrymple misjudged it, and it went over his head. Curt Welch and Doc Bushong raced around to score and Latham stopped at third. Now the game was all tied up at 3–3.

The St. Louis Globe-Democrat reported:

"The demonstrations on the part of the spectators when the score was tied was such that has never been equaled at any game of baseball before. The immense crowd seemed to go crazy. They yelled and cheered until they grew hoarse. Men and boys shook hands and embraced each other, turned somersaults on the grandstand and in the field, and many actually wept tears of joy. The air was full of hats, handkerchiefs and umbrellas."

Caruthers bounced to third to end the inning.

NINTH INNING. Neither team scored in the ninth inning, but there was some excitement when Tip O'Neill sent a long drive to right field. "It looked to be good for two bases," wrote *The Globe-Democrat*, "but Ryan jumped for it and made one of the most remarkable catches ever seen on the grounds."

With the score tied at 3–3 after nine, the game became the first extra-inning contest in World Series history.

TENTH INNING. Once again Bob Caruthers sent Chicago down in order.

Curt Welch was the first St. Louis hitter in the bottom of the tenth. One run would win the championship, and he wanted to get on base badly. Clarkson threw a pitch inside, and Welch leaned into it so it hit him on the shoulder. He jogged happily to first base.

King Kelly and Cap Anson immediately jumped up in

Curt Welch led off the tenth inning with a single to center.
He was at third with one out when John Clarkson uncorked a wild pitch.
Welch broke for home and made his $15,000 "slide." (NBL)

protest, claiming that Welch let the ball hit him on purpose. Umpire Pierce thought it over for a few moments and decided the White Stockings were right. He ordered Curt Welch back to the plate.

It didn't seem to bother Welch. On the next pitch, he lined a single to center. Runner on first, nobody out. The winning run was on base.

Dave Foutz was the next batter. He hit a weak grounder to the left side. It looked like a double-play ball, but shortstop Ned Williamson booted it. Runners on first and second, nobody out.

The winning run—Curt Welch—was on second now, and Yank Robinson bunted the ball to advance Welsh to third. Runners on first and third, one out.

Doc Bushong was up. He was a weak (.223) hitter. Welch took a long lead from third.

"Clarkson, who is usually so cool, was visibly nervous," wrote The Globe-Democrat. "He rolled and twisted the ball around in his hands several times before he got in position to pitch it."

Clarkson finally got himself set and went into his windup. But the tension had ruined his usual pinpoint control, and the ball sailed over catcher King Kelly's head.

Welch took off from third base the instant the ball was past Kelly. He dashed home and scored the winning run. After trailing for almost the entire game, St. Louis had won it, 4 to 3. The Browns were the World Champions and the crowd was going crazy.

The Globe-Democrat described the scene:

"More than half of them made a grand rush for the players, yelling and making all manner of noises and demonstrations. As soon as they would run up against a man in the Browns' uniform they would throw him upon their backs and carry him off the field. The entire nine were taken to the dressing room in this manner. At various places in and around the park a crowd would congregate, and when someone would propose three cheers for the championship, they would be given with a will. Everybody was happy and everybody wanted to shake hands with everybody else."

The newspaper added: "The Chicagos packed up their bats and got off the grounds as quickly as possible."

About a third of the crowd hung around until the players came out of their dressing room. When each of the Browns emerged, he was surrounded by fans and cheered heartily. It wasn't until after dark that Sportsman's Park was quiet.

What Happened Afterward

The White Stockings didn't parade out of the ballpark in an open, horse-drawn buggy. They slinked out of town, disgraced. On the train leaving St. Louis, only the conductor knew the sad group was a team of ballplayers.

"They made a mournful-looking crowd, that reminded one more than anything else of a delegation of undertakers," *The Globe-Democrat* reported gleefully.

♦ The gate receipts from the World Series totaled nearly $15,000, and Curt Welch's dash to home plate with the winning run became known as "the $15,000 Slide." Baseball history books commonly refer to the game this way, but there's no evidence that Welch slid home.

The Globe-Democrat described the final play like this:

"He finally delivered [the pitch], but it was far over Kelly's head. The latter made no effort to get it, and like the other members of the team, stood in a half dazed manner and watched Welch come in with the deciding run."

If Curt Welch *did* slide, he was just hot-dogging, and the newspaper didn't consider it important enough to mention in their recap of the game.

♦ Another St. Louis newspaper, *The Republican*, called the game "the greatest contest ever known to the history of baseball." They couldn't resist taking a poke at the White Stockings by saying, "Chicago should confine itself to the slaughter of hogs as a popular amusement. Baseball seems to require more headwork."

♦ To give you an idea of how newspapers covered sports in 1886, this was all one out-of-town paper—*The New York Times*—had to say about the game: "Ten innings were played, the score standing: St. Louis 4, Chicago 3."

♦ After the game, St. Louis Browns owner Chris Van Der Ahe sent a note to White Stockings president Albert Spalding suggesting their two teams play an exhibition game in Cincinnati the following Tuesday.

Spalding replied with a telegram: "We must decline. . . . We know when we have had enough." Spalding was so disappointed with the way his players performed that he refused to pay their train fares home from St. Louis.

◆ Von Der Ahe gave $580 to each of his players and kept the rest of the $15,000. He had a banner made that read, ST. LOUIS BROWNS, CHAMPIONS OF THE WORLD.

◆ The next season, St. Louis first baseman Charlie Comiskey became the first baseball player to endorse a product—Menell's Penetrating Oil.

Comiskey would later become a manager, and in 1900 he bought the Chicago White Stockings (then called the White Sox). It is Comiskey who often gets the blame for baseball's "Black Sox" scandal, when his 1919 White Sox threw the World Series. He vastly underpaid his players, making them vulnerable to gamblers.

◆ In 1887, "spring training" was born when Cap Anson took the White Stockings to Hot Springs, Arkansas, to get in shape for the upcoming season. Anson also developed the idea of a "pitching rotation" (having a staff of pitchers take turns). In 1892 he campaigned to abolish the bunt, which he believed was an unfair and unmanly way to hit.

Cap Anson was so much a part of the White Stockings that when he left the team in 1897, they briefly became known as "the Orphans." Anson was still playing in the majors when he was 44 years old, and he hit .331 that season.

◆ Chicago sold John Clarkson and Mike "King" Kelly to the Boston Beaneaters the next season for the then-astonishing sum of $10,000 each.

Clarkson's catcher and close friend Charlie Bennett was run over by a train in 1893, and he lost both his legs. Clarkson was so upset that he retired from baseball. He finished with a 325–177 career record.

Kelly died from pneumonia at age 36. In the hospital, he fell off a stretcher onto the floor and joked, "That's my last slide." Those were his last words.

◆ St. Louis won the American Association pennant again in 1887 and 1888, making it four in a row for the Browns.

◆ The American Association collapsed due to financial problems in 1890, and St. Louis joined the National League. In 1901, the American League was formed.

◆ In 1899, St. Louis got new uniforms with red trim and red striped stockings. With that, the team got the name it uses today—the Cardinals.

◆ The White Stockings became the Colts in 1892 and the Cubs after the turn of the century. They wouldn't win another pennant until 1906.

◆ Arlie Latham was still playing when he was 49 years old. His career finally ended when he bet a teammate $100 he could throw a ball farther. Latham won the bet, but damaged his arm permanently.

He became baseball's first full-time coach in 1909, for the New York Giants. Later, he was an umpire and manager. In 1952, 92-year-old Arlie Latham was still in the game. He was the custodian of the New York Yankees' press box.

For Baseball Trivia Lovers . . .

♦ Hall of Famers who played in this game: Clarkson, Anson, Kelly, Comiskey. All four were inducted long after they'd passed away.

♦ Because of ragged fields and no gloves, baseball players made many more errors in those days. In this Series, Chicago made 34 errors, and St. Louis made 29.

♦ This was the dead ball era. Home runs were rare, and hitters didn't swing for the fences. As a team, St. Louis hit just 20 home runs in 1886. Chicago had 53.

♦ This was the first time a championship series was referred to as "the World Series" in *The Sporting News*.

♦ Mike "King" Kelly was known for bending the rules of the game whenever he could. With just one umpire watching the field, Kelly would often run from first base to third base without touching second if the ump wasn't paying close attention.

The most famous Kelly story involves a time he was the player/manager for Boston and sitting out a game. An opposing batter lofted a lazy foul ball toward the dugout. Seeing that his catcher had no chance to make the play, Kelly shouted, "Kelly, now catching for Boston!" and stepped out of the dugout to snare the ball. A rule was quickly put into effect banning substitutions while the ball was in play.

CHAPTER

6

The Houston Marathon

THE DATE: Wednesday, October 15, 1986.

THE PLACE: The Astrodome, Houston.

THE SITUATION: Game 6 of the National League playoff between the Houston Astros and the New York Mets.*

New York Met pitcher Jesse Orosco (NBL)

*Some readers may be thinking " '86 Mets? How can this book ignore the Bill Buckner game?"

True, Game 6 of the World Series, when the Red Sox were a strike away from winning it all and a grounder went through the legs of first baseman Bill Buckner, was a terrific game. It will be remembered for centuries, but I think *this* game was even *better*. Interested readers can find "The Buckner Boot" in my book *Baseball's Biggest Bloopers: The Games That Got Away* (Viking, 1993).

"Throw nothing but sliders," Carter instructed Orosco. "I'll call for other pitches, but just keep shaking me off to confuse them." (NBL)

walk a
Hatch

sing!
enly t
n eith
na. B
ders

ver

in
nth
6th
and
ing
en-

ant-
ore

Mets 7, As

ETS
                    ab r h b
lson cf   7 1 1
tchell lf   4 0 0
ster ss   3 0 0   C
rnandez 1b   7 1 1
rter c   5 0 2   C
rawberry rf   5 2 1   C
night 3b   6 1 1   2
utel 2b   3 0 1   C
ckman 2b   2 1 1   h
ntana ss   3 0 1   C
eo ph   1 0 0
cDowell p   1 0 0
hnson ph   1 0 0
osco p   0 0 0   0
eda p   1 0 0
zzilli ph   1 0 0
uilera p   0 0 0   0
rkstra cf   4 1 2   1

tal   54 7 11 6
ts   000
uston   300
Game-Winning RBI
E — Bass. DP — H
uston 5. 2B — Ga
awberry. 3B — Dy
— Doran (2). S — C

ts
eda
uilera
Dowell
osco W. 3-0
uston
epper
ith
dersen
ez L, 0-1
houn
Wild pitch — Calho
ocklander; First, h
rd, Pulli; Left, Re
2. A — 45,718.

Then the Met
run in the 14th. I
ing the pennar
rected thems
Hatcher hit a
Orosco. And fi

imactic game was "kind of bittersweet."

*7*HE AVERAGE BASEBALL GAME takes about two and a half hours. This one wasn't average.

The New York Mets and Houston Astros battled through 16 innings, nearly five hours of edge-of-your-seat baseball with the National League pennant on the line. It was the longest postseason game in history, and one of the most exciting.

THE METS AND ASTROS were both founded in 1962, and both teams struggled through years of lousy players and last-place finishes. By 1986, the Mets had won one World Series (1969) and lost one (1973). Houston had not won a single pennant.

In their twenty-fifth season, both teams roared to their division titles, the Astros by 10 games, the Mets by 21. It was a head-on collision for the pennant.

They split the first four games, and the Mets won a 12-inning thriller in Game 5 to take a 3–2 lead in the series. Game 6 was a "must win" for the Astros. If they lost, they would lose the pennant.

But it was a must win for the Mets, too. If they lost, they would have to face Houston's best pitcher—Mike Scott—in Game 7. The dreaded Scott had already beaten them twice, striking out 19 and giving up just seven hits and one run in 18 innings.

Scott threw a split-finger fastball, which umpire Doug Harvey described as "a fastball with a bomb attached to it." Scott, who once pitched for the Mets, used the pitch to lead the National League in ERA, strikeouts, shutouts, and innings pitched. He may have been the most important factor in Game 6, and he didn't even play in it.

"We didn't want to face Scott again," Mets catcher Gary Carter said nervously.

But then, the guy Houston had on the mound *today* was no pushover either. Left-hander Bob Knepper had won 17 games during the regular season, including three against the Mets.

For New York, the starting pitcher was Bob Ojeda, another left-hander. Ojeda *also* had a great season—18–5, 2.57 ERA—and he had beaten Houston 5–1 in Game 2.

Seven-year-old Amber Pennington warbled the national anthem, and the marathon was under way.

FIRST THROUGH EIGHTH INNINGS. Knepper retired the Mets easily in the first inning, but Ojeda had his problems. He was a breaking-ball pitcher, and some would call him a junkballer. Ojeda threw the ball so slowly that his best pitch was called a dead fish. It would mosey its way up to the plate and just sort of die there.

The dead fish wasn't dead enough. Bill Doran, the Houston second baseman, led off with single to center. Runner on first, nobody out. Doran had 42 stolen bases for the season, so Ojeda watched him carefully.

Center fielder Billy Hatcher was up next. He hit a grounder to first, and Doran was forced at second. One out.

Phil Garner, the Astros third baseman, slashed a double

to left field. Hatcher scored all the way from first and it was Astros 1, Mets 0.

That brought up rookie sensation Glenn Davis. In his first full season, Davis had slammed 31 home runs. Davis hit a homer off Dwight Gooden in Game 1, and the final score of that game turned out to be 1–0. He didn't hit the long ball this time, but Davis did single to center and Garner came around to score. Astros 2, Mets 0.

When Ojeda walked right fielder Kevin Bass on four pitches, Rick Aguilera quickly began warming up in the Mets bullpen.

Runners on first and second, with two runs in and one out. Lefty Jose Cruz, a six-time .300 hitter, kept things going with a single over first base. Glenn Davis scored, making it Astros 3, Mets 0.

Runners on first and third, and there was still only one out. It was looking like this was going to be the biggest blowout in postseason history.

Houston wanted more. Switch-hitting catcher Alan Ashby came to the plate with instructions to pull off a squeeze play—to drop a bunt while the runner on third ran home with the pitch. It's a risky move because if the batter *misses* the bunt, the runner on third is a dead duck.

Ashby missed the bunt. Mets catcher Gary Carter caught the pitch and whipped it to third to nail Bass. Two outs. Jose Cruz took second on the play, but he was stranded there when Ashby lined to short to end the inning.

At the end of one inning, the Mets were down 3–0, but it

could have been a lot worse. The failure to get that fourth run home would come back to haunt Houston.

"I was a little edgy," said Bob Ojeda, but he settled down after that disastrous first inning and didn't give up another run through the next four innings.

Meanwhile, Bob Knepper was cruising along. He retired the first seven Mets in a row. A walk and a single broke the streak, but then Knepper sent down another 14 Mets in a row.

After five innings Bob Ojeda was taken out and replaced by Rick Aguilera, and he pitched three scoreless innings.

After eight innings, Knepper was in command with a two-hitter and a comfortable 3–0 lead. The Houston bullpen was hittable, but the Mets hitters were having a tough time getting to hit against it. They had only nine hits in their last 29 innings.

The game seemed like it was in the bag for the Astros. With Mike Scott scheduled to pitch the next day, hopes were high in the Houston dugout.

But some Astros fans remembered what happened the *last* time Houston was this close to winning a pennant. In the 1980 National League pennant race, the Astros had a three-run lead going into the eighth inning of the final game. They lost.

NINTH INNING. In the Mets dugout, manager Davey Johnson had a headache. His team was three outs away from losing the game and 12 hours away from facing Mike

Scott for the pennant. The Mets pitcher, Rick Aguilera, was due to bat.

Johnson called little (five-foot eight-inch) left-handed Lenny Dykstra out to pinch-hit. Playing in his first full season, "Nails" had hit .295 and stolen 31 bases. He'd already won Game 3 with a homer in the ninth inning. Dykstra was—and is—a competitor. He's a singles hitter who loves to hit home runs.

"I knew what my job was," Dykstra said later. "Get on base somehow."

The Mets were down 3–0 in the ninth when Dykstra nailed a triple. (AP/Wide World Photos)

It was lefty against lefty. Knepper threw two strikes and two balls. On the next pitch, Dykstra threw his weight into the swing and launched a shot to right center. Billy Hatcher went back as quickly as he could, but the ball sailed over his head. By the time he chased it down, Dykstra was standing on third base.

There was new life in the Mets dugout. They remembered that in Game 3 Knepper had a four-run lead in the sixth inning, but the Mets came back and won.

"You could see the guys saying to themselves, 'Hey, we can hit this guy,' " said catcher Gary Carter.

Runner on third, nobody out. Mookie Wilson, another speedy singles hitter, stepped up to the plate. Knepper got two strikes on him, but then Wilson whacked a single off the leaping Bill Doran's glove at second base. Dykstra scored, and it was Astros 3, Mets 1.

A hush fell over the Astrodome. In the Houston bullpen, Dave Smith grabbed his glove and quickly began warming up.

Now the Mets' big guns were coming up.

Kevin Mitchell had escaped the streets of San Diego with three shotgun wounds before making the big leagues. As a rookie in 1986, he played six positions for the Mets and hit .277. Mitchell grounded out to third, but Mookie Wilson moved to second base on the play. The Mets were down to their last two outs.

Keith Hernandez was up. "Mex" had won the National

League batting title and MVP in 1979. This year he hit .310, fifth in the National League. Hernandez, a great clutch hitter, was the right man at the right time. On a 2–1 pitch, he slammed the ball to the base of the center-field wall for a double. Mookie Wilson scored. Astros 3, Mets 2.

It had looked hopeless for the Mets, but suddenly they had the tying run on second base with one out.

Houston's rookie manager Hal Lanier decided to pull Bob Knepper before the Mets could do any more damage. He brought in bullpen ace Dave Smith, who had saved 33 games for the Astros. Knepper received a standing ovation as he walked slowly off the field.

The batter was catcher Gary Carter. He was having a terrible series—just two hits in 22 at-bats—but both his hits had won games for the Mets.

Carter hung tough. He worked the count to 3 and 2, then fouled off two pitches to stay alive. The next one looked out of the strike zone, and Carter laid off it. Umpire Fred Brocklander agreed. Carter jogged to first. Dave Smith stormed around the mound, fuming.

Now the *winning* run was on base. Runners on first and second, one out. Darryl Strawberry was strolling to the plate.

If you're any kind of baseball fan, I probably don't have to tell you much about Straw. He hit 27 home runs in 1986, and 252 in his first eight seasons in the majors. With those long arms extended on a low outside pitch, balls would leap off his bat into the deepest regions of National League ballparks.

Like Carter, Strawberry was also having a lousy series (.227). So far in the game, he had struck out twice and grounded out. Straw bombed one of Smith's pitches into the upper deck, but foul. Like Carter, Strawberry worked the count until it was full. And like Carter, he walked.

Now Smith was *really* steamed. He thought the pitches to Carter and Strawberry were both strikes, and he should have been in the clubhouse pouring champagne over somebody's head. Instead, he was fighting to save the game.

Ninth inning. Bases *loaded*. One out. The tying run was on third and the winning run on second. The Astros needed a double play badly.

The batter was third baseman Ray Knight. Many fans thought the 34-year-old Knight was washed up a year earlier, but he came back and hit .297 for the Mets. Smith got two strikes on him and thought he had the third one, but Brocklander called the pitch a ball.

On the next delivery, Knight drove the ball 375 feet to right center-field. Kevin Bass caught it out there, but was too deep to make any play at the plate. Keith Hernandez tagged up after the catch and dashed home with the tying run. Astros 3, Mets 3.

As they say in baseball, it was a new ball game.

On Knight's fly ball, Gary Carter had advanced to third and Darryl Strawberry to second. Two outs. The Mets had the chance to put it away once and for all. A single would score two more runs.

The batter was switch-hitting second baseman Wally Backman. Backman had the best season of his career in 1986, hitting .320, so Houston walked him intentionally to load the bases.

That left it up to pinch hitter Danny Heep. Interestingly, it was Heep who the Mets received when they traded away Mike Scott in 1983. He was a lefty, and his four pinch-hit home runs had led the majors that year. It would have been fitting for Heep to get a hit and win the game to prevent Scott from pitching a Game 7.

Smith and Heep battled for five pitches, and it was another full count. Tie game. Ninth inning. Bases loaded. A whole lot of fingernails were getting chewed to the bone.

Had Heep connected, you would probably know his name before reading it here. But he struck out swinging. Three outs. With their backs against the wall, the Mets had bravely rallied to tie it up, but they could not push across the go-ahead run.

As he came out of the dugout to take third base in the bottom of the ninth, Ray Knight was so nervous, his legs were shaking.

THIS IS ONE GAME that really began in the ninth inning. Ojeda and Knepper were gone. It became a battle of the bullpens.

Roger McDowell came in to pitch the ninth inning for the Mets, and he sent the Astros down easily.

TENTH THROUGH THIRTEENTH INNINGS.
Larry Anderson came in for Houston, and the Mets couldn't touch him. McDowell fired five shutout innings, allowing just one single. It was the longest relief appearance of his career.

"How far are you going to go with Roger?" Mets pitching coach Mel Stottlemyre asked manager Davey Johnson.

"We're taking all he's got," Johnson replied. "We're saving nothin' for tomorrow."

Johnson was prepared to burn out his bullpen in an effort to win the game, because Mike Scott was sitting in the Houston dugout waiting for tomorrow.

As the tie game went into the thirteenth inning, it became the longest playoff game ever.

FOURTEENTH INNING.
Aurelio Lopez was the new Houston pitcher. Señor Smoke, as he was called, had pitched 12 seasons in Mexico. *The Baseball Encyclopedia* lists him at 185 pounds, but *Sports Illustrated* called him "the most out of shape pitcher ever to appear in postseason play."

Gary Carter started things off with a single to right. Strawberry walked. Runners on first and second, nobody out.

Ray Knight tried to bunt the runners over, but Lopez hustled off the mound and threw the ball to third for the force out. Runners were still on first and second, but now there was one out.

Wally Backman didn't waste any time. He liked the first pitch he saw from Lopez and lined a single to right. When Strawberry touched home plate, the Mets had their first lead of the game. Mets 4, Astros 3.

Lopez settled down after the hit and didn't allow the Mets to pile on any more runs.

NOW IT WAS THE ASTROS who had the pressure on. Three more outs and their season would be over. They hadn't scored in 12 innings, and the Mets bullpen hadn't allowed an earned run in 18 innings.

The Mets called on their closer, Jesse Orosco, to finish Houston off. Orosco threw fastballs and sliders that started outside to right-handers and broke late to catch the corner of the plate. He had been the winner of Game 3 and Game 5, allowing just one hit and no runs in five innings.

Orosco struck out Bill Doran swinging for the first out. Houston hearts were sinking when bubble gum–popping Billy Hatcher stepped up to the plate. A .258 hitter with just eight career homers, Hatcher was not a long-ball threat. When the count became 3–2, Houston was down to its last four strikes.

A beautiful thing about baseball is that anything can happen at any time. On any given day, the worst pitcher in the world might strike out a Babe Ruth. The worst hitter in the world might hit a home run off a Sandy Koufax. You never know.

With a full count, Hatcher took a rip at an Orosco fastball and nailed it far down the left-field line. The ball landed on the screen high up on the left-field foul pole. It was fair by less than a foot. Mets 4, Astros 4.

The Astrodome erupted. Once again, it was a new ball game.

Orosco could have easily fallen apart at this point, but he didn't. He got the next two hitters and the fourteenth inning ended with the score still tied.

By this time, it was rush hour on the East Coast. Word had gotten around New York City that the Mets were involved in an extra-inning pressure cooker game to decide the pennant, and rabid Mets fans were paralyzed.

Businesspeople refused to leave their office buildings because they didn't want to miss the ending on the way home. People on the street were glued to the windows of appliance stores watching the game, just like baseball fans had done in the days when few people had TV sets at home. Viewers watching at home dashed to their refrigerators and bathrooms between innings so they wouldn't miss a single pitch.

SIXTEENTH INNING. Neither team had scored in the fifteenth inning, and the tension mounted. The game was well into its fourth hour. Darryl Strawberry led off the sixteenth with a bloop into center field off Aurelio Lopez.

Billy Hatcher made a desperate effort to make the catch, but the ball bounced high off the Astroturf and Strawberry was safe at second.

Ray Knight was up. He had driven in the crucial tying run in the ninth inning. It was an obvious sacrifice situation.

"Do you want me to bunt?" Knight asked Mets manager Davey Johnson.

"No," Johnson replied. "I want you to drive the ball to right field."

Knight did as he was told, singling sharply to right. Strawberry came around to score the go-ahead run. Mets 5, Astros 4. Knight took second on the throw to the plate.

Wally Backman was up. He had driven in the go-ahead run with a single in the fourteenth inning.

That was all for Lopez. Houston manager Hal Lanier came out and brought in left-handed sinkerball specialist Jeff Calhoun. The previous season, Calhoun had pitched 20 consecutive scoreless innings.

Calhoun didn't have it. He threw a wild pitch to Backman, sending Ray Knight to third base. Calhoun couldn't find the plate, and walked Backman. Runners on first and third, nobody out, with the pitcher due up.

Davey Johnson would have liked to pinch-hit for Jesse Orosco, but the Mets bullpen was shot. The previous game had gone 12 innings. The Mets needed Orosco to pitch the bottom of the sixteenth.

Orosco was instructed to try and squeeze a run home with a bunt. But he didn't have to. Calhoun threw *another* wild pitch, and Ray Knight raced home as the ball squirted behind the plate. Mets 6, Astros 4. Backman took second on the wild pitch. Orosco then sacrificed him to third.

Lenny Dykstra came up with a runner on third and one out. Dykstra ripped a single to right, and now the score was Mets 7, Astros 4.

At last it looked like one team had gotten the upper hand in this game. Even though Mookie Wilson hit into an inning-ending double play, the Mets' lead seemed safe.

BUT IT WASN'T. Orosco managed to strike out Craig Reynolds on fastballs, but he walked the veteran Davey Lopes and gave up a single to Bill Doran. Runners at first and second, one out.

The tying run was at the plate—Billy Hatcher, who had homered in the fourteenth inning. "I was dragging," Hatcher said after the game. "My whole body was hurting."

Orosco was exhausted, too, but he was still throwing his fastball. Hatcher lined the first pitch into center field for a single, and Lopes scored. Mets 7, Houston 5.

Runners on first and second, one out. The tying run was on base, the winning run at the plate. Houston had blown a three-run lead in the ninth, then had come back from the brink in the fourteenth. In the sixteenth they were scraping to overcome a three-run deficit.

On TV, it looked like Jesse Orosco's face was twitching. There was nobody warming up in the Mets bullpen. It was Orosco's game to win or lose.

By this time, the entire nation realized a baseball classic was in the making.

The Mets held a meeting on the mound.

"Shoot, get somebody out," Ray Knight told Orosco desperately.

"Kid," Keith Hernandez said to catcher Gary Carter, "if you call another fastball, I'll kill you."

Orosco switched to his slider, and Denny Walling hit one on the ground to first. Hernandez scooped it up and threw to second to get the force play on Hatcher. Two outs. Bill Doran advanced to third base.

Houston was down to its last out, but they had runners on first and third with Glenn Davis at the plate. Davis, you remember, hit 31 homers in the regular season and one in the playoff. He was the one Astro capable of putting one in the seats at any time.

"Play deeper!" third baseman Ray Knight shouted to rookie shortstop Kevin Elster. Just a few weeks earlier, Elster had been called up from the minors. He had played in 19 major-league games, and was sent into the middle of this game to pinch-hit for the Mets' regular shortstop, Rafael Santana. What a way to start your major-league career.

Elster backed up behind the white line, but Davis didn't hit the ball to him. He singled to center. Doran trotted home from third and incredibly, it was a one-run game *again*. Mets 7, Astros 6. The Astrodome was going crazy.

Runners on first and second, two outs. The tying run would come around on a single. A double or better would win the game for Houston, but any kind of an out would lose it for them. And the pennant with it.

Kevin Bass was up. He hit .311 for the season, and was hitting .304 in the series with three two-hit games.

The game was four hours and 42 minutes old at this point. It was 7:48 P.M. New York time.

Gary Carter went to mound to talk to Jesse Orosco. He knew Orosco's fastball had deserted him a few innings back.

"Throw nothing but sliders," Carter instructed the pitcher. "I'll call for other pitches, but just keep shaking me off to confuse them."

"The game is in your hands," Ray Knight whispered to Orosco. "You've got to be the one. Do it, Jesse, do it."

To himself, Orosco repeated, "We're only one out away. Gut it out."

A strike. A ball. A ball. A strike. A ball. Full count.

Bass and the Astros were down to their last strike of the season.

A hit could win the game.

The runners at first and second got ready to take off with the pitch.

Carter flashed a series of meaningless signs, and Orosco got ready to throw his sixth straight slider.

Swing and a miss!

The game was over and the New York Mets had won the National League pennant. There would be no tomorrow, and there would be no Mike Scott to come in and save the day for Houston.

Orosco hurled his glove in the air triumphantly. If you look at the highlight video, you see it go up, but you never see it come down.

"I think my glove must be still up there on the roof somewhere," Orosco said after the game.

What Happened Afterward

New York City went crazy, as the Big Apple has a tendency to do. The floodlights on the Empire State Building were blue and orange, the colors of the Mets.

♦ A few postgame quotes:

Ray Knight, who drove in the tying run in the ninth inning and the go-ahead run in the sixteenth: "This is my sixteenth year in professional baseball, and I've never been involved in anything so emotional or been under such mental strain."

Kevin Bass, who struck out to end the game: "I'm very teed off. It couldn't have been a better situation. I felt great up there. I had the vision of getting a hit. His big pitch is the breaking ball, and it's a tough pitch to hit. I was gearing for just one fastball. But I never saw one. I saw nothing but breaking balls. He beat me."

(Bass was acquired by the New York Mets in 1992.)

Bob Knepper, Houston's starting pitcher: "I never wanted a game so bad, for the team and myself. I did well for eight innings tonight, but then I just fell apart. It's going to be a long winter."

(Knepper went 8–17 the next season.)

Davey Johnson, Mets manager: "I was scared to death. I

was scared they were going to come back one more time."

◆ The Most Valuble Player of the series was Mike Scott.

◆ In the World Series, the Mets lost the first two games at home to the Boston Red Sox, but came back to win dramatically in seven games. Ray Knight was the World Series MVP.

◆ The next season Darryl Strawberry and Howard Johnson became the first teammates in baseball history to both hit 30 home runs and steal 30 bases. The Mets finished in second place. HoJo had another 30–30 season in 1989.

◆ Houston outfielder Billy Hatcher was suspended for ten days in 1987 when his bat split open and umpires saw it had been corked. Mike Scott was also accused of cheating on many occasions, but was never caught or punished.

◆ Within three seasons, almost the entire Mets team had scattered. Ray Knight and Kevin Mitchell were gone in 1987. Mitchell won the MVP and led the San Francisco Giants to the National League West title. Wally Backman and Jesse Orosco were gone in 1988. In 1989, Mookie Wilson, Keith Hernandez, Gary Carter, Lee Mazzilli, Rick Aguilera, Roger McDowell, Lenny Dykstra, and manager Davey Johnson were traded, released, fired, or became free agents.

The Mets have become famous for their bad trades, the worst of which sent 24-year-old Nolan Ryan to the California Angels for Jim Fregosi in 1971.

◆ Mets left-hander Bob Ojeda severed the middle finger of his pitching hand while clipping the hedges outside his house in 1988. The tip of his finger was reattached at a crooked angle so he would be able to throw his curveball. He came back and won 13 games in 1989. He joined the Los Angeles Dodgers in 1991 and went 12–9.

♦ In 1993, Ojeda was nearly killed in a boating accident that took the lives of two of his Cleveland teammates.

♦ In 1992, former Houston pitcher Aurelio Lopez was killed in an automobile accident. He was 44.

♦ As this book goes to press, the Houston Astros have yet to win their first pennant.

For Baseball Trivia Lovers . . .

♦ The New York Mets hit .189 as a team in this series, and it was only the second time a team has hit under .200 and won. The Mets struck out 57 times in the six games, with Darryl Strawberry fanning 12 times in his 22 at bats. As hitters in the first three innings, the Mets were 2 for 57.

But their pitching was sensational, and they only made one error in six games. The Mets won three of their four victories in their final turn at bat.

♦ The longest postseason game before this one was Game 2 of the 1916 World Series. Boston and Brooklyn struggled through thirteen innings at 1–1 until the Red Sox pushed across another run in the bottom of the fourteenth. The winning pitcher was 21-year-old Babe Ruth, who pitched all 14 innings.

♦ In his playing days, Mets manager Davey Johnson played second base for the Baltimore Orioles. He made the last out in the 1969 World Series against the Mets.

In 1973, Johnson played for Atlanta, and the Braves became the only team to have three players hit 40 home runs in one season. Johnson hit 43, Hank Aaron hit 40, and Darrell Evans hit 41. Even so, the Braves came in fifth place.

Davey Johnson played two seasons in Japan, and became the only player to be a teammate of both Hank Aaron and Japanese home-run champ Sadaharu Oh.

◆ Hall of Famers who played in this game: As this book goes to press, none. Many of the players are still active. But Gary Carter, Keith Hernandez, Darryl Strawberry, and Kevin Mitchell have a shot at Cooperstown.

◆ The first indoor, air-conditioned baseball game took place on April 9, 1965, the day the Astrodome opened. Mickey Mantle got a single on the second pitch of the exhibition game that day, and he hit the first indoor home run a few innings later.

With the Astrodome came the most dramatic changes in baseball since the game began. Outfielders no longer had to gauge the wind. Rain delays and rainouts were obsolete.

Most importantly, it was the Astrodome that brought us artificial turf. During the first few games, there was natural grass under the dome, but outfielders had trouble following fly balls among the 4,596 Lucite panels on the roof. The outside of the dome was painted to correct the problem. The natural grass inside the Astrodome died, and an era of baseball died with it.

◆ Mookie Wilson's real name is William Hayward Wilson. From 1983 to 1985, he hit .276, .276 and .276.

CHAPTER
7

The Homer in the Gloamin'

THE DATE: Wednesday, September 28, 1938.
THE PLACE: Wrigley Field, Chicago.
THE SITUATION: The Pittsburgh Pirates held
a half-game lead over the Chicago Cubs going into
the last weekend of the season.

Gabby Harnett, the Cub catcher/manager (NBL)

LEAD LIFE'S BIGGEST *
was the THRILL?—JUST
bs' ninth
ght victory ASK HARTNETT

Harnett crosses the plate after hitting his "homer in the gloamin'."
(AP/Wide World Photos)

ingle by Paul Waner. Hartnett won
the battle
n To Down Bucs first time si

*N*OT THAT LONG AGO, baseball was played on real grass under warm sunshine. Nowadays, nearly all major-league games are played at night beneath powerful lights. Many of them are played in domed stadiums with artificial turf and air conditioning.

It doesn't matter which way the wind outside is blowing—there *is* no wind inside. No grass stains. Outfielders never lose the ball in the sun. The sun doesn't matter.

Back in the days of day games, the sun sometimes played a crucial role in baseball. Games were often called on account of darkness. If it was all tied up and the sun was dipping below the bleachers, the umpires would have to decide if it was too dark to continue play. For safety's sake, when a pitcher is throwing a baseball 90 miles per hour, it's important that the batters can see it.

Flipping on the stadium lights was not an option at Wrigley Field in 1938. There *were* no stadium lights.

The setting sun played a major role in the dramatic finish of the following game. Today, more than 50 years later, they're still talking about it in Chicago. The day after the game, *The Chicago Daily News* called it "one of the most dramatic baseball games in history."

THE PITTSBURGH PIRATES looked like they had a lock on the National League pennant in 1938. Early in the season they peeled off 13 victories in a row, and their record was 40 wins and 14 losses through July. The Chicago Cubs were in distant second place and going nowhere. Anticipating a trip to the World Series, the Pirates management constructed a new press box in Forbes Field that would seat 600 reporters.

On July 20 it was announced that the Cubs' catcher of 17 years—Gabby Hartnett—would take over as manager of the team. Hartnett was a big, moonfaced man with a jolly laugh and the complexion of a tomato. They called him Gabby because he rarely said anything.

But somehow, Gabby woke the Cubs from their summer hibernation. As soon as he was appointed manager, the Cubs started winning.

Meanwhile, the Pirates went into a September swoon. The hitters either hit the ball right at somebody or they didn't hit at all. The pitchers were suddenly ineffective.

At the beginning of September, Pittsburgh had a seven-game lead. On September 9, the lead was down to three and a half games. With just six games left in the season on September 27, the Pirates pulled into Chicago for a three-game series. Pittsburgh was in first place by a game and a half, but the Cubs had won seven in a row and 17 of their last 20.

In the first game of the series, the legendary Dizzy Dean beat Pittsburgh 2–1, despite a fading fastball and a sore arm. That put the Cubs just a half a game behind Pittsburgh. The second game in this series is the one baseball fans will remember as long as there *is* baseball.

FIRST INNING. Clay Bryant (19–11) was the starting pitcher for the Cubs. He threw the ball hard, but like many power pitchers, he didn't always know where it was going. Bryant led the National League in both strikeouts and walks.

In the first inning, Bryant walked three Pirates hitters, but a double play erased two of them and kept Pittsburgh off the scoreboard. Bryant was looking shaky.

Pittsburgh took the field in the bottom of the first with rookie Bob Klinger (12–5) on the mound. He retired the Cubs without too much difficulty.

SECOND INNING. Klinger nailed down the first two outs in the second, bringing up James "Ripper" Collins. Ripper had some power. He led the league with 35 home runs in 1934.

But that's not how he got his nickname. When he was a boy, he hit a ball that landed on a nail in a fence and ripped off the cover. From that day forward, James was Ripper.

Ripper singled, making the first hit of the game.

The next Cub hitter was Bill Jurges, the team's light-hitting shortstop. Klinger fanned him for what would have been the third out of the inning, but the ball squirted away from catcher Al Todd. By the time Todd got hold of it, Jurges was standing on first base.

Runners at first and second, two outs.

That brought up the pitcher, Clay Bryant. He hit a roller

down the third-base line. Lee "Jeep" Handley scooped it up cleanly, but his throw to first was wild. Ripper Collins came around to score and it was Cubs 1, Pirates 0.

THIRD THROUGH SIXTH INNINGS. Bob Klinger was pitching masterfully but his defense was collapsing around him. By the end of the fourth inning, the Pirates added a passed ball, a dropped fly, and a botched peg to the wild throw.

The Cubs loaded the bases in the third inning, but couldn't score. Neither team could push across a run in the fourth or fifth inning.

Clay Bryant was working on a one-hitter when he came out to face the Pirates in the sixth. He got the first two hitters, and then Pirates left fielder Johnny Rizzo came to the plate. Rizzo was having a terrific rookie season, hitting .301 with 23 homers and 111 RBIs.

Bryant let fly, and Rizzo liked what he saw. The ball went soaring over the left center-field wall for a home run. Cubs, 1, Pirates 1.

The home run rattled Clay Bryant. He walked first baseman Gus Suhr and second baseman Pep Young. Arky Vaughan beat out an infield hit.

Bases loaded, two outs. There was frantic warmup action in the Cubs bullpen.

Jeep Handley was the next Pittsburgh batter, and he bounced a single up the middle. Vaughan and Suhr scooted home to make it Pirates 3, Cubs 1.

Pittsburgh catcher Al Todd was up next. The previous year Todd had his best season ever, hitting .307 with 86 RBIs.

Cubs manager Gabby Hartnett decided to lift Clay Bryant and bring in veteran reliever Jack Russell (6–1). Russell put out the fire by getting Todd to line out to second.

THE CUBS DIDN'T ROLL OVER and play dead in their half of the sixth. Gabby Hartnett, who was catching as well as managing the team, started things off with a double to the center-field wall. It might have gone for a triple, but Hartnett was not the fastest runner in the game, and he stopped at second base.

It didn't matter, because Rip Collins immediately smashed a double off the right-field wall. Gabby scored easily, making the score Pirates 3, Cubs 2.

Billy Jurges was up, and he beat out a bunt for a base hit. Now the Cubs had runners at first and third with nobody out.

Hartnett sent up Ken O'Dea, a lefty, to pinch-hit for the pitcher. O'Dea popped out, which prevented Collins from coming home from third base with the tying run.

The next Cub batter was Stan Hack, the third baseman. They called him Smiling Stan. Hack was just a singles hitter, but he hit a *lot* of them. His batting average was .320 for the season.

Hack whacked a grounder into the hole at second base. Pep Young made a good play stopping the ball and throwing to first for the out, but Rip Collins scored. Pirates 3, Cubs 3. Billy Jurges reached second on the play.

Next up was future Hall of Famer Billy Herman. A lifetime .304 hitter, Herman topped the .300 mark eight times. He slammed a hard grounder into the hole between third and short.

Billy Jurges took off from second base. He saw the ball go past and thought it was sure to go through the infield. If he hustled, he thought, he could score the go-ahead run on the single.

Just one problem—the ball *didn't* make it past the infield. Pittsburgh shortstop Arky Vaughan stopped it.

Not seeing Vaughan glove the ball, Jurges rounded third and was chugging home. Catcher Al Todd was waiting at the plate for the throw.

Al Todd was not a mountain of a man at six foot one and 198 pounds, but he was tough. The previous season Todd didn't allow a single passed ball. He was most famous for an incident in the minor leagues when he punched out Dizzy Dean.

So Todd wasn't exactly shaking in his boots when 175-pound Bill Jurges came storming down the third-base line. The throw was there five feet ahead of Jurges. His only hope was to crash into Todd and knock the ball loose.

As Jurges smashed into him, Todd threw him a hip and a shoulder. Jurges went flying, landing heavily. Todd held the ball. The umpire's thumb went up to indicate an out. Jurges was still lying in the dirt, dazed.

"It was quite a while before he was able to sit up and take an interest in things," reported *The Chicago Herald Examiner.*

Jurges recovered and stayed in the game. It was still tied up at 3–3 going into the seventh inning.

SEVENTH INNING. Rookie Vance Page (5–4) came in to pitch for the Cubs. With two Hall of Famers due up, he had his work cut out for him.

They were the Waner brothers, Paul and Lloyd. Paul was a slugger, and known as Big Poison. He won the National League batting title in 1927 (.380), 1934 (.362), and 1936 (.373). Lloyd (Little Poison, of course) was no pushover either, with a .316 lifetime average.

With one out, Lloyd Waner singled. His brother Paul followed with another single, putting Pirates runners at first and third. The batter was Johnny Rizzo, who had clouted a home run in the sixth inning. The Cubs infield hoped for a ground ball and moved into double-play position.

Vance Page went into his windup, and hesitated for a moment before releasing the ball. The umpire was about to call a balk, but Rizzo swung at the pitch. The ball was up around his ears, and he slapped a hard grounder toward third.

Stan Hack scooped it up and threw to second for one out. Pep Young relayed it to first for an inning-ending double play. The Cubs ran off the field happily and the Pirates ran on, screaming to the umpires that a balk should have been called on Page.

The umps could not be convinced. It was getting late in the afternoon and they wanted this game to move along before it became dark.

The Cubs didn't score in their half of the inning and the score remained tied going into the eighth.

EIGHTH INNING. Vance Page was still on the hill for the Cubs, and he would have two more future Hall of Famers to deal with this inning.

The first was Joseph Floyd Vaughan, nicknamed Arky because he came from Clifty, Arkansas. Vaughan was hitting .329 coming into the game, third best in the National League. Three years earlier he'd had a career year, winning the MVP and leading the league by hitting .385. That was 32 points higher than the runner-up (Joe Medwick).

Arky only struck out 21 times all season, while walking 104 times. No wonder pitchers were so careful with him. Page tried to get Vaughan to bite at pitches off the plate, but Arky knew the strike zone like he knew his name. With ball four, he trotted to first.

Lefty Gus Suhr singled, and the Pirates were threatening again with runners on first and second with nobody out.

Manager Gabby Hartnett went to his bullpen, bringing in lefty Larry French (10–19) to replace Vance Page. Pittsburgh manager Pie Traynor (also a Hall of Famer) responded by summoning 16-year-veteran Heinie Manush off the bench to pinch-hit for Pep Young.

When he was a young player, Manush had big shoes to fill. He replaced the immortal Ty Cobb in center field for the Detroit Tigers in 1926. He did it in grand fashion, too, hitting .378 and winning the American League batting title. Manush was no Cobb, but he would hit .300 or better 11 times.

Now he was 37 and hanging on as a pinch hitter. Manush did his job, rapping a single. Arky Vaughan scored from second, and Pittsburgh jumped into the lead once more, 4–3.

Hartnett didn't waste any time going to his bullpen again. If he didn't win this game, the Cubs would be a game and a half back and possibly out of contention. He brought in Big Bill Lee, who had pitched a full nine innings two days earlier and one inning the day before.

General Lee, as he was often called, led the league in wins (22) and ERA (2.66). Fans could recognize his pitching motion by his extremely high leg kick.

Jeep Handley was up for Pittsburgh. He didn't care about how many wins Lee had or how high he kicked his leg. He only wanted to keep the rally going. Handley smacked a single, and Gus Suhr scored. Pirates 5, Cubs 3. Heinie Manush was on third now.

Chicago's hopes for a pennant were fading as quickly as the daylight.

Al Todd rapped a grounder to short and Bill Jurges threw

home to nail Manush for the first out of the inning. A double play got the Cubs out of further trouble, but they were down by two runs with time running out.

IN THE BOTTOM OF THE EIGHTH, Ripper Collins led off for the Cubs with a single, his third hit of the afternoon.

Bob Klinger had been pitching a great game, but Pittsburgh manager Pie Traynor decided he'd had enough. Bill Swift, a sidearm fastballer, marched in from the bullpen.

Swift swiftly walked Bill Jurges. The tying run was on base for the Cubs. It was the pitcher's turn to bat, and it was obvious that a pinch hitter would be called on. This could be Chicago's last chance to pull it off.

From the Cub dugout climbed Tony Lazzeri. You'll read more about him in the next chapter, but for now it's enough to say that Lazzeri had been a longtime New York Yankees slugger who joined the Cubs at the start of the season. He only batted 120 times, for a .267 average.

Runners on first and second, nobody out. Lazzeri was instructed to sacrifice the runners into scoring position. He tried to lay down the bunt, but the ball trickled foul. Strike one. Lazzeri tried again, and once more the best he could do was foul the ball off. Strike two.

As you probably know, if a hitter bunts the *third* strike foul, he's out. So the bunt sign was taken off and Lazzeri was instructed to swing away.

That's what he did, and the ball shot off on a line to right field. Paul Waner couldn't catch up with it. Ripper Collins scored, making it Pirates 5, Cubs 4. Bill Jurges made it to third, and Tony Lazzeri was standing on second with a double. Still nobody out.

Now the wheels were beginning to turn in the managers' heads. Lazzeri represented the winning run on second base. He was not a fast runner and might not be able to score on a single. Cubs manager Gabby Hartnett brought in the speedier Joe Marty to pinch-run for Lazzeri.

With Cubs runners on second and third and nobody out, Pirates manager Pie Traynor decided to have Stan Hack walked intentionally. That would set up a force out at any base. Pirates infielders would be able to suck up a ground ball and throw it home to choke off the tying run.

But it didn't work out that way. The always-dangerous Billy Herman rammed a single through the infield. Bill Jurges scored easily to tie the game up at 5–5.

Joe Marty had been brought into run for Tony Lazzeri, and that's what he did when Herman hit the ball. He ignored third-base coach Red Corrigan, who was shouting to hold up, and raced for the plate. Marty was determined to score the go-ahead run.

It was a reckless play on Marty's part. It might have made sense to try for home if there had been two outs, but with nobody out Marty should have stopped at third base and given one of his teammates a chance to drive him in. Even a long fly ball would bring in the important run.

That apparently hadn't occurred to Joe Marty, for he was heading for the plate like a fire engine heading for a blaze.

Pirates right fielder Paul Waner scooped up the single and gunned it home. The throw was true and Al Todd slapped the tag on Marty. Out!

Instead of having the bases loaded with nobody out, Chicago had runners at first and second with one out. The possible game-breaking rally was completely choked off when Mace Brown came in to pitch for Pittsburgh and got Frank Demaree to hit into an inning-ending double play.

It was a big blown opportunity for the Cubs. But at least they had tied up the game.

By this time, it was starting to get dark outside. The umpires gathered to discuss the situation. If it had been the beginning of the season, they probably would have called the game on account of darkness right then and there. But this was a crucial game for both teams, and there weren't many days left for makeup games.

The umps decided that one more inning would be played. If the score was still tied after nine innings, the two teams would play a doubleheader the following day.

NINTH INNING. Having gone through five pitchers, the Cubs were just about out of arms. Hartnett brought in another old-timer, 39-year-old Charlie Root. It was Root who was pitching for the Cubs when Babe Ruth hit his famous "called shot" home run in the 1932 World Series. He won 26 games back in 1927, but his glory days were long past.

Root rose to the occasion. He got Lloyd Waner on a fly

ball to right for the first out. Paul Waner ripped a single to left, but Johnny Rizzo popped out. Arky Vaughan was at bat when Lloyd Waner tried to steal second. Gabby Hartnett whipped the ball across the diamond and gunned him down for the third out.

IT HAD BEEN A GRUELING AFTERNOON. The Cubs had gotten off to a lead, lost it, tied the game, fallen behind, and tied it again. Now it was the bottom of the ninth, and Chicago had one last chance.

Mace Brown was Pittsburgh's best pitcher. One of first players to be used mainly as a reliever, he appeared in 51 games in 1938. He won 15 of them and lost 9.

The first hitter he faced was Carl Reynolds, a six-time .300 hitter. Mace was throwing the ball as hard as he could to take advantage of the growing darkness. Reynolds grounded out. One out.

Phil Cavarretta was up next. He got hold of a Mace fastball and hit a screamer to straightaway center field. Lloyd Waner pulled it down in front of the wall. Two outs.

STEPPING UP TO THE PLATE was Gabby Hartnett, catcher and manager of the Cubs. Born in Woonsocket, Rhode Island, just before Christmas of 1900, Gabby was playing in his seventeenth straight season with Chicago.

He'd had some great years. In 1930 he hit .339 with 37 homers and 122 RBIs. In 1935, he hit .344 and won the

National League's Most Valuable Player award. Just the previous season he'd hit for his highest average ever—.354. And he would finish his career with 236 homers.

With two outs in the bottom of the ninth, it was all up to Gabby to get something going.

"Darkness was blotting out the playing field," reported *The Philadelphia Inquirer.* "It was obvious that if Hartnett couldn't come through somehow the game would have to be called."

Mace Brown pulled his cap down and hitched his belt up. He decided to abandon his fastball strategy and get Hartnett out with low curveballs.

Gabby looked at the first one, and the umpire called it a strike.

Brown threw another low curve and Gabby took a swing at it, but the only thing he hit was air. Strike two. The Wrigley crowd groaned.

Hartnett wasn't looking good. He was down to his last strike. It was so dark, fans in the outfield seats could hardly see the field, much less the ball.

With a two-strike count, Mace Brown would have been expected to stall, waste a few pitches out of the strike zone in hopes that Gabby might chase one. After all, time was on Brown's side.

The Earth doesn't care about baseball. It keeps rotating no matter who's winning or what inning it is. With each passing second, day was turning into night in Chicago.

But Brown threw a third curveball, this time a bit higher on the outside part of the plate. Gabby was in no position to be choosy. He lashed at it.

The crack of the bat told the crowd that wood had struck ball. It was so dark, it was impossible to tell where the ball was heading or how far. There was a moment of silence.

Suddenly, there was a roar from the left-field bleachers. The fans in that part of the ballpark got up on their feet, not to stretch their legs, but to reach out for the most famous home run in Chicago Cubs history. Game, set, match.

The third-base umpire confirmed everyone's suspicions, and Wrigley erupted. Newspapers, scorecards, and hats flew on the field.

After being nine games behind the Pirates a little over a month earlier, the Chicago Cubs were in first place with just three games left in the season. The final score was Cubs 6, Pirates 5.

Gabby Hartnett had taken matters into his own hands and won the game with one mighty swing of his bat. It seemed like a corny happy ending to a movie, but it was really happening.

As he rounded first, Gabby was joined by a few delirious Cubs fans. When he reached second there was a crowd, including his teammates. He couldn't even *see* third base. That's where Dizzy Dean was, hopping up and down like a madman and windmilling his arms.

By that time Gabby was no longer running—he was swept along by the momentum of the crowd around him.

The Chicago Daily News wrote: "As he came around the base and turned toward third, his stomach all shaking like Santa Claus', his face one great smile, his eyes looked up out over the rocking, screeching, tossing grandstand to the twilight sky, where low over the top of the grandstand— and over his left shoulder—hung the new moon."

More than a hundred frenzied Cubs fans were surrounding Gabby, and stadium ushers were swinging their fists trying to get them off the hero of the day. Hartnett's uniform was just about torn off. Home plate umpire George Barr watched carefully to see that Hartnett's foot touched the plate.

Mace Brown brushed his hand across his eyes and walked off the field, his head bent over. The Pittsburgh fielders stood in their places, too stunned to walk off the field. They'd been in first place for ten weeks. One *pitch* ago they were in first place. Now they were in second, and maybe out of the race.

What Happened Afterward

"I figured Brown for a curve on that 0–2 pitch, and I got set," Gabby said while puffing a cigar after the game. "I swung with everything I had, and then I got that feeling— the kind of feeling you get when the blood rushes out of your head and you get dizzy.

"A lot of people have told me they didn't know the ball was in the bleachers. Well, I did—maybe I was the only one in the park who did. I knew it the minute I hit it. It was the most wonderful thing that ever happened to me."

Mace Brown, the losing pitcher, said, "I threw three curveballs to Hartnett, and I would do the same today. The curveball was my best pitch, and I gave Hartnett my best pitch."

◆ A Chicago mailman named A. R. Westra caught the ball and fought off dozens of other fans trying to grab it from him. After the game he made his way to the locker room and asked security guards to have Gabby sign the ball for him.

"Give me that ball," Hartnett said. "I want to keep that thing as long as I live."

He got a fresh baseball, wrote his name on it and gave it to the mailman. Hartnett lived until 1972.

◆ Hartnett's blast came to be called the Homer in the Gloamin'. The word *gloaming*, which we don't hear much anymore, means "twilight" or "dusk."

◆ The next day, Bill Lee pitched for the fourth day in a row, and the Cubs crushed the demoralized Pirates 10–1 to sweep the series and extend their lead to a game and a half.

Chicago clinched the pennant a day later.

◆ The good fortune of the Cubs didn't carry over into the World Series. The New York Yankees trounced them in four straight games. Gabby Hartnett went 1 for 11 at the plate (.091) with no homers.

◆ In honor of the game's losing pitcher, the new press box that had been constructed in Pittsburgh for the anticipated World Series came to be called Mace Brown's Folly.

◆ Gabby Hartnett went on to manage the Cubs two more years. They finished fourth and fifth. Hartnett joined the New York Giants in 1941 and hit .300. It was his last season.

◆ Pittsburgh traded Arky Vaughan for four players after the 1941 season. He drowned at age 40 in 1952 when his fishing boat capsized.

◆ The only pennant the Chicago Cubs have won since the Homer in the Gloamin' was in 1945, when most of the best baseball players were fighting World War II.

◆ In 1988 Wrigley Field became the last major-league ballpark to install lights. There will never be another Homer in the Gloamin'. When it gets dark now, they just flip a switch and keep playing.

For Baseball Trivia Lovers . . .

◆ Gabby Hartnett played a part in another great moment in baseball history. He was behind the plate in the 1934 All-Star game when Carl Hubbell struck out Hall of Famers Babe Ruth, Lou Gehrig, Jimmy Foxx, Al Simmons, and Joe Cronin consecutively.

◆ The three "old" men of the Cubs who were the heroes of this game—Tony Lazzeri, Charlie Root, and Gabby Hartnett—had nearly 50 years of major league experience between them.

◆ Hall of Famers who participated in this game: Paul and Lloyd Waner, Vaughan, Manush, Hartnett, Herman, Lazzeri, Traynor.

◆ In 1933, when he was with the Washington Senators,

Little Poison and Big Poison. Lloyd and Paul Waner patrolled the Pirate outfield together from 1927 to 1940. Each weighed less than 150 pounds, but both could pound a baseball. Lloyd hit .300 ten times. Paul did it 14 times. The Waner brothers combined for 5,611 career hits, 1,300 more than Pete Rose.

Heinie Manush became the first player thrown out of a World Series game. He pulled on umpire Charley Moran's bow tie and let it snap back in the ump's face.

◆ Pittsburgh first baseman Gus Suhr started a streak of 822 consecutive games in 1931. The streak was broken in 1937 when he missed a game to attend his mother's funeral.

CHAPTER
8
The Alexander Game

THE DATE: Sunday, October 10, 1926.
THE PLACE: Yankee Stadium, New York City.
THE SITUATION: Game 7 of the World Series
between the New York Yankees
and St. Louis Cardinals.

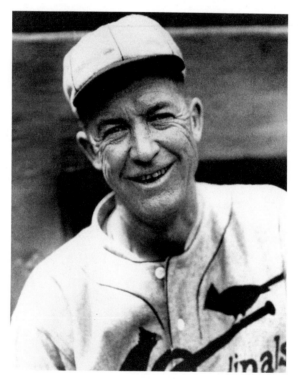

Grover Cleveland Alexander (NBL)

Legend has it that Alexander was asleep in the bullpen when he was called in to face Tony Lazzeri with the bases loaded. It became the most famous pitcher/batter confrontation ever. (NBL)

*W*HEN THE NAME GROVER CLEVELAND ALEX-
ander is mentioned to serious baseball fans, they almost
always think of the final game of the 1926 World Series.
Even though Alexander the Great only faced seven batters in
a relief appearance, his stint on the mound is remembered
as one of the most dramatic moments in baseball history.

Alexander was one of 11 brothers brought up on a farm
in Elba, Nebraska. He learned to pitch, at least according
to legend, by throwing rocks at chickens.

One day in 1910, a scout for the Philadelphia Phillies
discovered him while looking over another Nebraska pros-
pect named George Chalmers. The club decided to take a
chance on Alexander, too, acquiring him for $750.

It paid off many times over. In his rookie season, Grover
Cleveland Alexander led the American League in wins (28),
complete games (31), innings pitched (367) and shutouts
(7). From 1915 to 1917, he won 30 games or more each
season.

He became known, along with Walter Johnson and
Christy Mathewson, as one of the finest pitchers in the game.
He had a pinpoint fastball, a sidearm curve, and he could
change speeds on both pitches easily.

"His fastball sneaked," Hall of Famer Frank Frisch once
said. "You'd get set, but it would be by you, in the catcher's
mitt. He mixed his pitches like nobody before or since."

IN 1926 ALEXANDER WAS 39, pitching in his sixteenth
season, and suffering from the first sore arm of his life. It

looked like his career in baseball was through. He was 3–3 with the Chicago Cubs when they released him in the middle of the season.

But Alexander wasn't quite finished. The St. Louis Cardinals picked him up, and he won nine games for them, a big reason the Redbirds made it to the World Series. It was in this World Series, against Babe Ruth, Lou Gehrig, and the New York Yankees, that Grover Cleveland Alexander had his finest moment.

THREE DAYS BEFORE THE SERIES was to begin, Rogers Hornsby's mother passed away. Hornsby was the manager and second baseman of the Cardinals. As his mother lay dying in Texas, he told her he wanted to stay with her, but she encouraged him to go play in the World Series. Her last words were, "Stay with your team and win."

The Yankees were heavy favorites, but Alexander made them look like a bunch of bush-leaguers by tossing complete game victories in Game 2 and Game 6. Herb Pennock was the star pitcher for the Yankees, winning Game 1 and Game 5.

After six games, it was all tied up at three games apiece. The winner of Game 7 would be the winner of the World Series. St. Louis had never even won a *pennant* before, much less a World Series.

Not every home had a radio in 1926, so loudspeakers were set up in the streets of St. Louis to blast the play-by-play. Crowds gathered around, choking off the traffic.

After Alexander won Game 6, Hornsby said to him, "You're in the bullpen tomorrow." Having gone nine innings on Saturday, there wasn't much chance he would have to crank up his old "soupbone" again on Sunday.

"All right, Rog," replied Alex. "But I'll tell you, I'm not going to warm up in the bullpen. I've got just so many throws left in this arm. I'll take my warmup pitches on the mound."

FIRST INNING. It was an awful day in New York. Announcer Graham McNamee of WJZ radio told his listeners, "It is cold. It is dreary. It is dark. It is dripping. It is damp and thick and all that, but it doesn't make any difference. You can't dampen the ardor of a real baseball fan."

The winning pitchers of Games 3 and 4 faced each other in the final game—Waite Hoyt for the Yankees and Jesse "Pop" Haines for the Cards. They both looked sharp, and neither team scored in the first two innings.

THIRD INNING. The knuckleball is a funny pitch. It flutters to the plate slowly and veers this way and that as the air buffets against the seams of the ball. It can be maddeningly difficult to hit. Jesse Haines was a knuckleballer, and one of the best.

Most knuckleballers, despite the name of the pitch, grip the ball with their fingertips. Haines actually held it with his *knuckles*. He sent down Yankees center fielder Earle

Combs and shortstop Mark Koenig easily in the third inning, bringing the immortal Babe Ruth to the plate.

Ruth was a 13-year veteran at the time and had hit 356 of his 714 career home runs. He almost single-handedly won Game 4, slamming three round trippers.

Here's the call of Graham McNamee on WJZ radio: "Again the crowd is cheering Babe Ruth as he comes up to the plate. He digs his right foot into the ditch right near the plate. His body pivots at the waist as he swings, and he gets tremendous leverage. Before he hits the ball, he gets a half swing of the body. No wonder the ball travels when he hits it. Ball one. Strike one. The crowd is yelling and booing Haines for pitching him a ball.

"Here it is—a long drive into the right field, and—*a home run!* There you are, a long drive into the right-field bleachers, making the score 1–0 in favor of the Yankees, amidst a terrific noise. Babe Ruth comes in after a slow jogging trip around the circuit, bows, and takes off his hat to the crowd."

That's the tough part about throwing knuckleballs—they don't always knuckle. The ball soared over an enormous razor-blade advertisement and landed in the bleachers.

That was all the scoring through the first three innings.

FOURTH INNING. Cardinals skipper Rogers Hornsby led off with a high grounder back to the box, and Hoyt threw him out at first. One out. Next up was first baseman Jim

Bottomley, who slapped the first pitch—a high fastball—into left field for a single. Runner on first, one out.

This is when a comedy of errors began for the Yankees. Hoyt threw a low curveball to Cardinals third baseman Lester Bell, who hit a routine grounder to short. It looked like a sure double play. But Mark Koenig, the rookie shortstop who led the league in errors with 52, played the ball to the side instead of getting in front of it. He managed to knock it down but couldn't make a play anywhere. Mistake number one.

Runners on first and second, one out. It was Koenig's fourth error of the World Series.

Errors happen, and Waite Hoyt shook it off. He got two strikes on the Cardinals left fielder Chick Hafey, and on the next pitch Hafey lifted a "Texas League" blooper to short left field. Koenig drifted back for it. Bob Meusel, the left fielder, came in. It was Meusel's play to make, but the two Yankees couldn't make up their minds who should take it. Both men stepped aside and the ball dropped between them. Mistake number two.

Now the bases were loaded with one out. The bloop was scored a single, but it should have been an easy out.

Things got worse for the Yankees. The National League's Most Valuable Player, catcher Bob O'Farrell, hit a fly ball to left center. The catch could have been made most easily by center fielder Earle Combs, but Bob Meusel dashed over from left field and waved Combs off the ball. Meusel had a better throwing arm, so there was a better chance he could throw out the runner on third if he tried to tag up after the catch.

That is, if there *was* a catch. In his haste to throw to the plate, Meusel botched the play. The ball bounced off his glove. Mistake number three.

Bottomley trotted home to tie the game up at 1–1. And the bases were *still* loaded with one out.

There was stunned silence in Yankee Stadium. The champions of the American League weren't supposed to muff easy plays.

Hoyt must have been fuming, but he kept his composure enough to get two strikes on Cards shortstop Tommy Thevenow. But Thevenow hit the next pitch into right field for a single. Les Bell and Chick Hafey raced around to score.

Cards 3, Yanks 1. All three St. Louis runs had been "kicked" across the plate, as they used to say in those days. The next two Cards went down, but the damage was done.

The Yankees hit the ball hard in the bottom of the fourth inning, but some good defensive plays kept them off the scoreboard. Nobody scored in the fifth inning.

SIXTH INNING. Jesse Haines was pitching well for the Cardinals, but a small blister had appeared on the middle finger of his pitching hand that was making it difficult for him to throw his knuckleball. He didn't tell anyone about it, and when he sent down Lou Gehrig and rookie second baseman Tony Lazzeri, it seemed like the blister wasn't a big problem. But Yankees third baseman Jumpin' Joe Dugan ripped a single to left center on a full count.

Next up was the catcher, Hank Severeid. He also ran the count full, which only made Haines's blister more inflamed. On the next pitch Severeid hit a line drive to left field. Left fielder Chick Hafey could have played it safe and picked up the hit on a bounce, but he went for a shoestring catch instead.

He missed it. The ball bounced over his head, and Dugan came all the way around from first to score. Cards 3, Yanks 2.

Severeid was on second with a double. Yankees manager Miller Huggins pinch-hit Ben Paschal for pitcher Waite Hoyt, but Paschal bounced out to end the inning.

SEVENTH INNING. The Yankee Stadium crowd cheered in appreciation when Herb Pennock came in to pitch. The Yankees hurler had already won two games in the World Series. He calmly sent down the Cards in the top of the seventh inning.

But time was running out on the 1926 season for the Yankees. They were down by a run with just three innings left.

Earle Combs stepped up to the plate. The Yankees' fans got up on their feet and cheered for a rally. Combs responded by hitting a high curveball to the left side. Thevenow, the shortstop, leaped as high as he could, but the ball ticked off his glove. Runner on first, nobody out. The tying run was on base.

Mark Koenig came to the plate and Babe Ruth to the on-deck circle. Upon instructions from Yankees manager Miller Huggins, Koenig dropped down a sacrifice bunt to advance Combs to second. Runner on second, one out.

As Babe Ruth walked up to home plate, the St. Louis infield gathered for a conference on the mound. Should they walk Ruth intentionally? That would set up a double-play situation and take the bat out of the slugger's hands. On the other hand, it would put the winning run on base with Bob Meusel (.315) and Lou Gehrig (.313) coming up.

The fans were howling for Ruth to hit a home run. But after allowing the big guy to hit four already, Cards manager Rogers Hornsby decided to let him have a base on balls.

The crowd booed lustily as four pitches sailed wide of the strike zone. Ruth tossed his bat away disgustedly. Clearly, walking was no fun for the Sultan of Swat. On his way to first, Ruth implored Meusel to get a hit.

The Cardinals seemed to have discovered Babe's only weakness—pitchouts. They would walk him 11 times in the seven-game series.

Runners on first and second, one out. Haines got two strikes on Meusel, and on the next pitch the left fielder hit a grounder to Les Bell at third. Bell flipped the ball to second to force out Ruth. Now there were runners at first and third with two outs.

Sharp baseball fans are probably asking, "Why didn't Bell step on third for the force play and then throw to first for an inning-ending double play?" That would have made sense. But lacking film or videotape of this World Series, we have no way of knowing if Bell was close enough to the third-base bag to make that play. (And Bell died in 1985.)

Lou Gehrig was the next batter. The Iron Horse was only in his second full season in 1926, but he was already a budding star. Haines got two quick strikes on him, but then threw four straight pitches off the plate for another walk.

Now the bases were loaded with two out, and Jesse Haines was having trouble getting his pitches over.

Catcher Bob O'Farrell walked to the mound to see what the problem was. Haines showed him the blister, which was now bleeding. Rogers Hornsby came over from his position at second base, and so did the rest of the Cardinal infield.

"Poosh 'em up Tony!" chanted Yankees fans. "Poosh 'em up!"

Standing at home plate was 23-year-old Tony "Poosh 'em up" Lazzeri. (The nickname meant "hit a homer.") This would be the last at-bat of his first year in the majors, a year in which he slugged 18 home runs, drove in 114 runs, and hit .275. Now he had the opportunity to break the game open and be the hero of the World Series. A single would drive in two runs and put the Yanks in the lead.

The meeting on the mound concerned the condition of Jesse Haines's finger.

"Can you throw it anymore?" Hornsby asked the knuckleballer.

"I can throw the fastball," Haines replied, "but not the knuckler."

"Well, we don't want any fastballs to Lazzeri."

Now the crowd was chanting, "Make him pitch! Make him pitch!"

Hornsby raised his right hand to signal the bullpen behind the left-field bleachers. Haines was finished for the day, and the season. A relief pitcher would be coming in to pitch to Lazzeri.

IN THE BULLPEN, according to some accounts of this game, Grover Cleveland Alexander was fast asleep. After pitching a complete-game victory in Game 6, Alexander didn't expect to work the next day, so he went out and did some celebrating. He was sleeping it off when his teammates jostled him and told him Hornsby wanted him to come in and pitch.

"What, again?" Alexander asked, annoyed. He grudgingly picked up his glove and walked slowly out of the bullpen.

A hush fell over the crowd when a figure stepped out of the shadows of the bullpen and ambled onto the field. He was wearing a red Cardinals sweater over his uniform.

"Who is it?" fans asked one another.

"Alexander!"

Alexander the Great may have gone nine innings the day

before, and he may have been exhausted and hung over, but he was the best the Cards had. If they're gonna beat you, baseball wisdom dictates, let 'em beat your best.

He looked like a gunslinger—his cap perched to one side, his left cheek slowly working a chaw of tobacco. His face was freckled and weather-beaten, his uniform rumpled.

Nothing seemed to faze Alexander. He was walking into a bases-loaded, one-run situation in the seventh inning of the seventh game of the World Series, and he looked like he was taking a stroll in the park. Some observers said he walked just a little slower than usual to give the hitter more time to build up a case of nerves.

"Over the long stretch of left field he lumbered," wrote *The New York Times,* "his shoulders bent, his crooked legs wobbling, his shoulders drooping. He looked like an old man, bent with age."

When Alexander reached the mound, he casually tossed his sweater to a batboy. Grover Cleveland Alexander was a man of few words. The following conversation is reconstructed from columns in *The Cleveland Plain Dealer, The New York Times,* and other sources.

"Who's up?" he asked Hornsby.

"Lazzeri."

"How many out?"

"Two."

Alexander looked around to see Yankees standing on first, second, and third. "Bases filled, eh?" he asked Hornsby nonchalantly. "I guess there's nothing much to do except give Tony a lot of hell."

Hornsby looked Alexander in the eyes and asked, "Can you do it?"

"I can try," the veteran pitcher responded. "I'll tell you what I'm going to do. I'm going to throw the first one to him fast . . ."

"No, no," protested Hornsby. "You can't throw him a fastball."

"Yes I can," replied Alex. "If he swings at it he'll most likely hit it on the handle, or if he hits it good it'll go foul. Then I'm going to come outside with my breaking pitch."

Hornsby looked into Alexander's eyes again, then shook his head. "Who am I to tell *you* how to pitch?"

With that, the meeting on the mound broke up.

ALEXANDER TOOK JUST FOUR leisurely warmup tosses— he didn't want to waste one of the few pitches left in his right arm. He was 39 years old, just about mandatory re- tirement age for a pitcher. To give you an idea of their age difference, when Alexander came up to the big leagues, Tony Lazzeri was eight years old.

Here was perhaps the most dramatic pitcher/batter con- frontation in baseball history—Grover Cleveland Alex- ander, the grizzled veteran, versus Tony Lazzeri, the rookie sensation. The bases were loaded with two outs in a one- run game, with the championship of the world on the line.

Lazzeri nervously pawed the dirt near the plate. He had struck out in the second inning and again in the sixth. He didn't want to whiff again.

"The fans slid forward to the edge of their seats," wrote *The New York Times*. One reporter noted that Alexander yawned.

The first pitch was low and outside for a ball. Then Alexander hit the outside corner for a called strike one. That evened up the count.

The next pitch was high and inside, and Lazzeri jumped all over it. The ball rocketed off his bat, a long drive down the left-field line. If it stayed fair, it would be a grand slam home run.

It didn't. It curved foul and millions of Yankees and Cardinals fans took a breath.

Now the count was 1–2, and Alexander had the advantage. He served up a low breaking ball on the outside corner. With two strikes on him, Lazzeri knew he had to protect the plate and didn't have the luxury of seeing how the umpire would call the pitch. He swung awkwardly and missed for strike three.

Four pitches and the battle was over. The three Yankees dejectedly walked off the bases and the Cardinals group-hugged Alexander and pounded him on the back all the way to the dugout.

NINTH INNING. But the game wasn't over. Neither team scored in the eighth inning and the Cardinals went down in order in the top of the ninth. St. Louis hadn't scored since the fourth inning, but they didn't *have* to—they had the lead.

In the bottom of the ninth the heralded "Murderer's Row" of the Yankees were coming up for one last try against Grover Cleveland Alexander. If he could get past Earle Combs and Mark Koenig, the last batter of the season would be—who else? Babe Ruth.

Combs went down quickly. Alexander threw two strikes by him, and then the center fielder hit a hot grounder to third. Les Bell plucked it and threw him out. The same thing happened with Koenig. Two strikes, grounder to third. Two outs.

Babe Ruth was the last chance for the Yankees. They were one run behind, but one swing of Ruth's bat could tie it up. As you know, he'd already hit one homer in this game and four total in the Series. The wisest strategy might have been to intentionally walk Ruth, but that wasn't Grover Cleveland Alexander's style.

It was another classic confrontation between two men who were very possibly the best hitter and best pitcher in baseball history. It was fitting that it would happen with two outs in the bottom of the ninth of the World Series finale.

Ruth came to the plate swinging three bats aggressively. Alexander spat. Ruth tossed two of the bats to the side. The two stars hadn't faced each other since the 1915 World Series—11 years earlier, when Ruth was a pitcher.

As the reporters debated whether Alexander would walk the Babe, the old pitcher whipped in strike one. Ruth didn't move the bat off his shoulder. 0–1.

"He's pitching to him!" gasped more than one reporter. Ruth looked out at the mound, disbelieving. Alexander was treating the great Babe Ruth like just another hitter. What nerve! Ruth gripped the bat more tightly.

Alexander was pitching to Ruth, all right, but he was pitching carefully. He preferred to make a mistake and walk Ruth than to make a mistake that would let him hit the ball out of the park.

The next pitch was off the plate for ball one. 1–1. Ruth liked the next one and took a swing, but he fouled it off. 1–2. The Yankees were down to their last strike of the World Series.

Alexander wasn't in any rush to get home to Nebraska. He tried to tempt the Bambino with a pitch out of the strike zone, but Ruth wouldn't bite. 2–2. Alexander tried it again, and again Ruth wouldn't pull the trigger. 3–2. Full count.

"This is a duel," Graham McNamee told the radio audience. "There is electricity in the air."

Alexander went into his gawky windup once more and aimed for the lower outside corner. The pitch was an inch or two off the plate and Ruth had the presence of mind to lay off it. Ball four.

The Babe hesitated a moment before tossing his bat in the air and taking his base. It was his fourth walk of the game.

A mixture of catcalls and cheers came out of the stands. The Yankees fans were happy that Ruth hadn't struck out, but disappointed that he hadn't knocked one over the wall and tied the game up.

Bob Meusel was up, looking to make up for the fly ball he muffed in the fourth inning. Alexander pumped the first pitch over and Meusel missed it. Strike one.

Ruth edged off first, taking a bigger lead than would be expected. He wasn't known as a base stealer, but he *had* swiped 11 bases that season.

Ruth tosses his bat away disgustedly. Walking was no fun for the Babe. (NBL)

You can imagine what was going through Ruth's mind: He knew Alexander was concentrating on getting the hitter out and wasn't paying close attention to him. With two outs, there was little hope of a Yankees rally. If he could make it to second, he would be able to score on a single. His mind was made up.

When Alexander began his windup for the next pitch, Ruth took off.

Hornsby rushed over to cover second base.

Catcher Bob O'Farrell caught the pitch from Alexander and whipped it to second.

Ruth slid in feet first.

The throw from O'Farrell was dead on. Hornsby snatched it and put his glove between the bag and Ruth's sliding foot.

Out! Game over! Season over! The St. Louis Cardinals were the World Champions for the first time in their history!

As Babe Ruth lay in the dirt at second base, Grover Cleveland Alexander stuck his glove under his arm and walked off the mound as if it was quitting time at the factory. It was all in a day's work for Alexander the Great. The Cards mobbed him. The man who had been discarded like an old shoe by the Cubs had come back to win two games in the World Series and save the final game.

What Happened Afterward

The streets of St. Louis, usually deserted on Sunday, were suddenly thick with people and cars. Confetti fell from office buildings, even though offices were officially closed. People tied cowbells, stovepipes, and washtubs to the backs of their cars and rattled them through the streets. Sirens and whistles blasted. ALEXANDER FOR PRESIDENT banners appeared.

In the celebration, 30 people were injured and one killed—17-year-old William Troll was riding on the running board of a car when it was sideswiped by a trolley car.

◆ The St. Louis clubhouse was a madhouse. "Bats were thrown high in the air and the celebrants had to duck as they descended with loud crashes," reported *The New York Times*. (There was no television in 1926, so newspapers were quite descriptive.) "Gloves went scaling across the room to nobody cared where. Uniform shirts were tossed on high."

Poor Grover Cleveland Alexander received the brunt of the exuberance. According to the *Times:* "The veteran was in imminent danger of having his skull dashed against the open door of his locker on several occasions as groups of players grabbed him on either side and started pulling simultaneously and in different directions, making him the immobile center line in a human tug-of-war. He was rocked from side to side by the demonstrative squad; he was rolled backward and forward under the impetus of the demonstration and he was almost knocked down several times as he sought to stand erect."

"Look out for my dogs!" Alexander complained, meaning his feet. "Leave me alone, will you? I want to get downtown and put on the feedbag."

◆ Newspapers blamed the Yankees' defeat mostly on Mark Koenig (four errors) and Bob Meusel (one error). Thomas

Holmes, a reporter for *The Brooklyn Eagle*, said Koenig was responsible for three of the Yankees' four losses and had played as though ground balls "were going to bite him."

Holmes wrote, "Mark Koenig, who feebly impersonates a shortstop for the Yankees, and Lazy Robert Meusel, who should have paid office rent in left field for the seven games, were the Patsys of the climax."

Baseball historians are still arguing about whether Babe Ruth made a bonehead play in trying to steal second in the bottom of the ninth.

◆ Having fulfilled his mother's last request, Rogers Hornsby attended her funeral in Austin, Texas, the day after the World Series.

During the off-season, Hornsby was traded to the New York Giants. His batting average over the next three seasons was a spectacular .361, .387, and .380. Bob O'Farrell, who threw out Babe Ruth to end the Alexander Game, took Hornsby's place as manager of the Cards.

◆ While Hornsby went to Texas, Babe Ruth went to Essex Fells, New Jersey, to visit an 11-year-old boy. Johnny Sylvester had been suffering from a serious case of blood poisoning, and Ruth promised him he'd hit a homer in Game 4. As it turned out, Ruth hit *three* homers in the game. Sylvester recovered.

◆ Incredibly, just a few days after the World Series, Grover Cleveland Alexander was back on the mound, pitching an exhibition game in Omaha.

In fact, Alexander still had a few good years left in him.

He went 21–10 the next season as a 40-year-old and 16–9 the year after that. He was still winning ball games when he was 43, and he finished his career with 373 victories— third highest in baseball history. He would have won even more if he hadn't served in the Army for nearly all of 1918. Alexander pitched for semipro teams into his fifties.

♦ The next season the Cardinals finished in second place, a game and a half behind Pittsburgh. The Yankees went all the way, and many fans believe the 1927 Yankees were the greatest baseball team to ever take the field.

♦ After the most famous strikeout in baseball history, Tony Lazzeri went on to a sensational 14-year career. He hit .354 in 1929, and on May 24, 1936, he hit two grand slam home runs in one game. Lazzeri was inducted into the Hall of Fame in 1991.

In 1946, the year before he died, Tony Lazzeri was in his saloon when he told a reporter, "Funny thing but nobody seems to remember much about my ball playing except that strikeout. There isn't a night goes by without some guy leaning across the bar and bringing up the old question. Never a night."

♦ Grover Cleveland Alexander became a Hall of Famer back in 1939, a time when baseball idols couldn't make a living by writing their names on balls and bats and baseball cards.

"I can't eat tablets or nicely framed awards," Alexander said sadly.

A year after his induction at Cooperstown, Alexander was

reduced to a sideshow attraction at a flea circus museum on New York's 42nd Street. He demonstrated fastballs, curveballs, fadeaways, and sinkers for curious gawkers.

"He shows all these deliveries," reported *The New York Times*, "along with the sidearm 'slider' that struck out Lazzeri, and exhibits them about a dozen times each in an afternoon."

♦ Thirteen years after the Alexander Game, Lou Gehrig took himself out of the Yankees' lineup after playing 2,130 consecutive games. He was diagnosed with amyotrophic lateral sclerosis, a rare and incurable disease. Gehrig died two years later, two weeks before his thirty-eighth birthday. ALS came to be known as Lou Gehrig's disease.

♦ In 1952, a movie about Grover Cleveland Alexander entitled *The Winning Team* was released. Ronald Reagan portrayed Alexander. So the great pitcher was named after one U.S. president (Grover Cleveland) and played by another.

In the movie, the 1926 World Series ended with Alexander striking out Lazzeri. In reality, he whiffed Lazzeri in the seventh inning.

For Baseball Trivia Lovers . . .

♦ When Alexander and Lazzeri had their famous confrontation, very few people were aware that the two men shared something in common—epilepsy. In 1917, toward the end of World War I, Alexander had been drafted and sent to France, where exploding shells cost him hearing in one ear and triggered the problem.

◆ In the minors in 1909, Alexander was hit between the eyes with a ball while trying to break up a double play. He was unconscious for two days. He woke up with double vision, and it was months before he could play ball. When Alexander came back, his first pitch broke three of the batter's ribs.

◆ Grover Cleveland Alexander won 373 games in his career, the third highest number of any pitcher. He was second highest in shutouts (90), had nine 20-win seasons, three 30-win seasons, and played for 20 years.

◆ In the record books, Alexander and Christy Mathewson each have 373 victories. But when they retired, Alex had 373 and Matty had 372. Years later, baseball historians looked at Mathewson's games closely and awarded him another victory.

◆ Rogers Hornsby didn't smoke or drink, and he was so concerned about weakening his batting eye that he wouldn't even go to the movies. Maybe it worked—Hornsby hit .424 in 1924, the highest single-season batting average of the twentieth century.

◆ This game was jam-packed with Hall of Famers: Alexander, Hornsby, Ruth, Pennock, Lazzeri, Gehrig, Hoyt, Haines, Bottomley, Huggins, Hafey, and Combs.

◆ Grover Cleveland Alexander was *not* the winning pitcher of the Alexander Game. Jesse Haines was. With the exception of his first big-league game (with the Cincinnati Reds in 1918) Haines pitched his entire 18-year career with the Cardinals.

His plaque in the Hall of Fame includes the only negative reference to another player on a plaque in Cooperstown. It reads: "He won 1926 World Championship for Cardinals by striking out Lazzeri with bases full in final crisis at Yankee Stadium."

♦ Bob Meusel's brother Irish Meusel was also a big-league ballplayer. The Meusel boys faced each other in three straight World Series when the Yankees played against the Giants in 1921, 1922, and 1923.

♦ Chick Hafey, the Cardinals left fielder, got the first hit in the history of the All-Star game in 1933.

♦ Ben Paschal, who pinch-hit for the Yankees in the sixth inning, has the distinction of being one of the only players in baseball history to pinch-hit for Babe Ruth. What happened was that Ruth whacked a home run in the ninth inning of a game and then the rest of the Yankees batted around. When it came time for Ruth to bat *again* in the same inning, he was nowhere to be found. So Paschal got the call.

♦ Lou Gehrig hit .295 his first full season, and he hit .295 his last full season.

♦ George Chalmers, the pitcher the Phillies were scouting when they stumbled upon Grover Cleveland Alexander, also made it to the majors. He wasn't nearly as successful. Chalmers pitched seven years for the Phillies, winning 29 games and losing 41.

CHAPTER
9
The Gibson Game

THE DATE: Saturday, October 15, 1988.
THE PLACE: Dodger Stadium, Los Angeles.
THE SITUATION: Game 1 of the World Series
between the Los Angeles Dodgers
and Oakland Athletics.

Kirk Gibson (NBL)

The Dodgers were down by a run in the bottom of the ninth.
Tommy Lasorda gave Gibson a shove up the steps.
He limped out of the dugout, barely able to walk. (NBL)

about it, this was the World Series

With Glory of the
West,

*K*IRK GIBSON WOKE UP on the morning of October 15 the way he often did—in pain. He tried to jog a little in his living room, but it was hopeless. His legs were killing him.

Gibson was the National League's Most Valuable Player, having hit .290 with 25 home runs and 31 stolen bases to lead the Los Angeles Dodgers to the western division championship. He was the hero of the playoffs with two home runs, one of them a twelfth-inning blast that demoralized and defeated the New York Mets.

But he played the entire playoff series with a pulled hamstring in his left leg. In the final game, he slid into second base and sprained a ligament in his right knee. When the World Series began, Gibson could barely get up from a chair.

THE DODGERS WEREN'T EXACTLY A POWERHOUSE that could afford to lose Kirk Gibson. They hit .248 as a team. A third of the opening-day roster had been on the disabled list sometime during the season. The year before they had finished fifth, losing 15 more games than they won.

But somehow, with timely hitting, a lot of heart, and the spectacular pitching of Orel Hershiser, the Dodgers managed to finish first in the National League West and upset the Mets in seven games to win the pennant.

Sportscaster Bob Costas called the Dodgers lineup "perhaps the weakest in World Series history." And that was *with* Kirk Gibson's bat.

The Oakland A's *were* a real powerhouse. Behind the pitching of Dave Stewart and Dennis Eckersley, Oakland led the American League in ERA and saves. With superstar sluggers Jose Canseco and Mark McGwire, they scored 800 runs (the Dodgers scored 628) and hit 156 homers (99).

Canseco and McGwire were known as "the Bash Brothers" because they would bash forearms after hitting home runs. Together they bashed 74 homers and drove in 223 runs.

Oakland blew past the Boston Red Sox in four straight games to win the American League pennant, and they were heavily favored to beat the Dodgers in the World Series.

"Our game is more well-rounded than the Dodgers," said Jose Canseco, both confident and cocky. "We've got better hitters, we've more power, more speed. I'd say we're a more qualified team. We're on a roll, we're enthused, and we've got lots of confidence."

Canseco predicted Oakland would win the Series in five games.

"We shouldn't even be on the same field with the Athletics," admitted Dodgers manager Tommy Lasorda. "The whole team scares me."

If being on the same field with the A's scared Lasorda, he must have been *terrified* when Kirk Gibson came to him before Game 1 and said, "There isn't anything I can do for you."

With that, Gibson limped into the trainer's room and got

a shot of cortisone to ease the pain in his aching legs. He didn't bother putting on his uniform. He'd watch the game on TV.

FIRST INNING. It was a balmy 75 degrees in Los Angeles. Pop singer Debbie Gibson belted out the National Anthem. Kirk Gibson (no relation to Debbie) wasn't introduced as the rest of the Dodgers took the field. He was lying on a training table in the Dodgers clubhouse.

Nancy Reagan threw out the first ball, a soft lob to Dodgers catcher Mike Scioscia. The 1988 World Series was under way.

Rookie Tim Belcher was called on to start the Series for Los Angeles. Dodgers manager Tommy Lasorda would have gone with his ace Orel Hershiser (23–8, 2.26 ERA), but Hershiser had pitched the final game of the playoffs just two days earlier. He would be pitching Game 2.

Belcher was actually signed out of high school by Oakland, but he was traded to Los Angeles before he reached the majors. He won 12 games for the Dodgers in his first full season and lost only 6. Four of those victories came in crucial September games, and he won two more in the playoffs. That convinced Tommy Lasorda that Belcher could handle the pressure of opening the World Series.

But maybe he *couldn't*. After striking out Carney Lansford, Belcher gave up a single to center by Dave Henderson and hit Jose Canseco on the right forearm. Runners on first and second, one out.

The dangerous Dave Parker, playing in his sixteenth season, flied out to center field. Belcher then walked Mark McGwire, who had slammed 32 home runs during the regular season.

Bases loaded, two out. Belcher was having trouble finding the plate, and the A's had the chance to jump in front right from the beginning. But Belcher got Oakland catcher Terry Steinbach to hit a fly ball to center field, and the Dodgers were out of the inning without giving up a run.

In the trainer's room, Orel Hershiser joined Kirk Gibson to keep the slugger company.

DAVE STEWART WALKED to the mound to pitch the bottom of the first. While Tim Belcher had started his career with Oakland and became a Dodger, Dave Stewart had started *his* career with the Dodgers and became an Athletic.

He had little success for five years, then blossomed when he was traded to Oakland—his hometown—and won 20 games in 1987 and 21 in 1988. He hadn't pitched off the mound in Dodger Stadium in five years.

Dodgers second baseman Steve Sax stepped up to the plate to start things off. Moments later he was lying in the dirt, the victim of a first-pitch fastball off his shoulder.

Umpire Doug Harvey immediately marched to the mound and warned Stewart that any pitcher suspected of throwing beanballs would be ejected from the game. It seemed obvious that Stewart had hit Sax in retaliation for Jose Canseco getting hit by a pitch in the top of the inning. After

Harvey's warning, both pitchers knocked it off, and no more batters would be hit by a pitch for the rest of the game.

Runner on first for the Dodgers, nobody out. Sax had stolen 42 bases for the year, and he was an aggressive base-runner. In trying to hold him on, Stewart was called for a balk, and Sax trotted over to second base. Franklin Stubbs, a left-handed hitter, flied to center field for the first out.

That brought up Mickey Hatcher, who was playing left field for the Dodgers while Kirk Gibson was injured. Hatcher was known more for his enthusiasm and dugout cheerleading than for his playing ability. He'd hit just one home run all season.

But the World Series is often filled with unlikely heroes. Stewart got one strike on Hatcher and then threw a pitch that Hatcher deposited over the blue fence in left center-field for a home run. Los Angeles 2, Oakland 0.

Instead of leisurely jogging around the bases, Hatcher sprinted as if he was trying to catch a bus.

"I just haven't ever had to develop a home run trot," he would explain after the game.

After Hatcher's clout, Stewart took care of the rest of the Dodgers to end the inning.

SECOND INNING. Tim Belcher's strategy was to keep Oakland's little guys off the bases so the big guys wouldn't be able to do too much damage. Unfortunately, he started off the second inning by giving up a single to second baseman Glenn Hubbard.

Belcher struck out rookie Walt Weiss, but then he committed the unspeakable baseball sin of walking the opposing pitcher. When Dave Stewart took ball four, he became the first pitcher to draw a World Series walk in seven years. It was all the more remarkable because Stewart, pitching in the American League, where they use the designated hitter, had not even been to bat in five years.

Nevertheless, Belcher gave him a free pass to first base, and then he walked third baseman Carney Lansford too. Oakland had loaded the bases for the second time in two innings. There was just one out, and the big guys were coming up.

The first big guy to take a crack at clearing the bases was Dave Henderson, who had come to the A's as a free agent that season. Hendu could hit the long ball. He hit .304 with 24 homers, 94 RBIs, and 38 doubles.

But with the pressure on, Tim Belcher reached back and struck out Henderson. The bases were still loaded, but now there were two outs.

That brought up Jose Canseco, probably the strongest and most exciting player in baseball that season. Just 24 years old, Canseco was having a spectacular year.

Before the season started, he said he would hit 40 homers and steal 40 bases, something *nobody* had *ever* done in the history of baseball. Canseco did it, hitting .307 and leading the league in home runs (42) and RBIs (124) and winning the American League MVP. To top off his terrific season, he slammed three home runs in the playoffs.

Canseco was truly dangerous with a bat in his hands.

AS CANSECO STEPPED TO THE PLATE with the bases loaded, the scoreboard flashed the fact that he had yet to hit a grand slam home run in his three years in the majors.

Jose took strike one, and on the next pitch hit a bullet— *rising line drive bullet*—to straightaway center field. It was over the fence even before Tim Belcher had the chance to turn around and watch it fly. The ball crashed into NBC's center-field camera 415 feet away from home plate, making a dent that Canseco would autograph the next day.

Grand slam! Oakland 4, Los Angeles 2. Canseco tossed the bat aside like it was a worn toothpick and trotted jauntily around the bases. All in a day's work.

Tim Belcher was rattled, and he walked Dave Parker. But he got Mark McGwire on a force play to end the inning.

SIXTH INNING. Dave Stewart settled down and didn't allow the Dodgers to score in the second, third, fourth, or fifth innings. Tommy Lasorda brought in Tim Leary (17–11, 2.91 ERA), who shut down the big bats of the A's for three innings.

In the bottom of the sixth inning, the Dodgers got back-to-back-to-back singles from Mike Marshall, John Shelby, and Mike Scioscia. The first single went to right field, the next to center field, and the third one to left field. That last hit scored a run, and the Dodgers crept back to make the score Oakland 4, Los Angeles 3.

SEVENTH INNING. Curveballer Brian Holton came in to pitch for the Dodgers. Oakland couldn't score off him.

In the bottom half of the inning the Dodgers threatened when Steve Sax singled and stole second, but his teammates could not bring him around.

IN THE DODGERS TRAINING ROOM, Kirk Gibson and Orel Hershiser were watching the game on TV. Announcer Vin Scully was talking about pinch-hitting possibilities for the Dodgers.

"The man who is the spearhead of the Dodger offense throughout the year, who saved them in the League Championship Series, will not see any action tonight, for sure," Scully told the TV audience.

Kirk Gibson pulled himself up off the training table. "Who *says* I can't hit?" he said. "I might be able to hit." He put an ice bag on his knee and painfully stretched his legs.

"Maybe he could hit," Hershiser said later, "but he sure was having trouble walking."

EIGHTH INNING. Once again Dave Stewart shut down the Dodgers, and Brian Holton kept Oakland's big guys *and* little guys off the bases. At the end of eight innings, the score was still Oakland 4, Los Angeles 3.

Some foolish Dodgers fans left the stadium, hoping to beat the notorious Los Angeles traffic. A true baseball fan, of course, stays at the game until the last out is made.

As the Dodgers were going down one, two, three in the eighth inning, Kirk Gibson pulled his uniform on. He picked up a bat and limped over to a batting cage under the stands.

The Dodgers' batboy, Mitch Poole, put a baseball on a batting tee and Gibson whacked it off, grimacing in pain as he swung. Poole put another one on the tee, and Gibson smashed that one off.

NINTH INNING. Alejandro Peña came in to pitch the final inning for the Dodgers. He gave up an infield single, but didn't allow the A's to score. Oakland had a 4–3 lead, but the Dodgers bullpen had shut them down since Canseco's grand slam in the second inning.

After hitting a bucket of baseballs off the batting tee, Kirk Gibson asked the batboy to go get manager Tommy Lasorda.

"Gibson wants to see you in the runway," Mitch Poole said to Lasorda as the Dodgers were coming off the field to hit in the bottom of the ninth.

Lasorda made his way under the stadium to Gibson, and the injured slugger simply said, "I think I can hit for you."

WITH A ONE-RUN LEAD going into the bottom of the ninth, Oakland manager Tony LaRussa always called on Dennis Eckersley, baseball's best relief pitcher.

Eck had been a starter for 12 seasons with Cleveland, Boston, and the Chicago Cubs before coming to Oakland in 1987. The A's made him into a reliever. In 1988 he saved 45 games, the most in baseball and one short of the major-league record. In the playoffs he saved all four games for Oakland.

Eckersley had a tricky sidearm delivery and nearly perfect control. He walked just 11 batters in 72 innings, and two of them were intentional walks.

THE DODGERS HAD THE BOTTOM of their order coming up to face Eckersley in the ninth inning. Catcher Mike Scioscia popped to second. One out.

Eckersley struck out Jeff Hamilton. Two outs. The crowd fell silent.

Kirk Gibson was in the dugout holding a bat, but Tommy Lasorda decided he wouldn't put him in the game unless the Dodgers got a man on base. Then he would bring Gibson in to try and drive in the tying run.

In the meantime, Lasorda hid Gibson in the corner of the dugout so Oakland wouldn't see him and adjust their pitching strategy.

Mike Davis, who was an Oakland A the season before, came out of the dugout to pinch-hit for the Dodgers. He had some pop in his bat. Davis hit 24 home runs in 1985 and 22 in 1987. Eckersley knew he had to be careful with him.

In the on-deck circle was Dodgers utility infielder Dave

Anderson. He was a light hitter with no power, and he hadn't played in two months.

It made sense for Eckersley to walk Davis and go after Anderson. But then again, it's never a good idea to put the tying run on base. And there was the chance that the Dodgers would pinch-hit for Anderson once Davis was on first.

Eckersley threw and Davis swung, fouling the ball off. Strike one. Eckersley threw a pitch out of the strike zone, and then another one. Two balls, one strike.

Davis stepped out of the batter's box to throw off Eckersley's timing a bit. Maybe it worked. Eckersley tossed in ball three and ball four too.

Dennis Eckersley, who hardly ever walked *anybody*, had walked Davis on five pitches and put the tying run on first base in the bottom of the ninth.

ALL EYES TURNED to the on-deck circle. Tommy Lasorda called Dave Anderson back into the dugout and gave Kirk Gibson a shove up the steps.

"Now go get 'em!" Lasorda shouted.

As Gibson hobbled to the plate, the crowd erupted with noise and rose to its feet. The fans knew Kirk Gibson was injured, but they didn't know how much pain he was in.

Gibson would say this after the game: "The way the crowd was screaming, the adrenalin kicked in, and I was able to forget a little bit about how much it hurt."

Vin Scully, the TV broadcaster whose words had made Gibson want to get on the field in the first place, told the viewers: "All year long they looked to him to light the fire, and all year long he answered the demands, until he was physically unable to start tonight with two bad legs."

The baseball fans of America couldn't help but think of *The Natural*, the 1958 book and 1984 movie about Roy Hobbs, an over-the-hill ballplayer. In the movie, Hobbs comes to the plate with two outs in the bottom of the ninth inning of the championship game. He's bleeding from his stomach, and the bloodstain goes right through his uniform. The movie ends with Hobbs hitting a miraculous homer to win the pennant.

The balding, limping Kirk Gibson didn't look much like Robert Redford, especially when he almost fell over swinging at Eckersley's first pitch. Gibson fouled it off.

"Tommy's got to get him out of there," thought Orel Hershiser in the Dodger dugout. "He doesn't have a chance."

Eckersley whipped another one over, and Gibson fouled it off too. Two strike count.

"Talk about a roll of the dice," said Vin Scully. "This is it."

WITH A RUNNER ON FIRST BASE, Gibson would have to hit at least a double to tie the game up. Lasorda flashed Mike Davis the steal sign. If Davis could make it to second, Gibson would only have to swing for a single.

Davis was running with the 0–2 pitch, a sinkerball. Gibson swung and topped it down the first-base line. He hobbled out of the batter's box, but the ball rolled foul. Gibson limped back to the plate, and Davis went back to first base.

Davis was running again with the next pitch. He had second base stolen, but Gibson fouled the ball back.

Captain Kirk limped around between pitches, bending his knee. At least he was swinging and getting a piece of the ball.

The next pitch was a slider that just missed the outside corner, and Gibson laid off it. Davis took off again and stole second without a throw.

NOW THE DODGERS COULD TIE the game up with a single. The pressure was off Gibson to get an extra-base hit. He just had to get one past the infield.

Eckersley threw another pitch out of the strike zone for ball two, and then another one for ball three.

Full count. Two outs. Bottom of the ninth. Runner on second. One-run game. Tense enough for you?

Oakland manager Tony LaRussa thought about walking Kirk Gibson intentionally to set up a force play at any base, but he knew Gibson was hurting and decided to go after him. The very healthy Steve Sax was on-deck.

The Dodgers scouting report on Dennis Eckersley said that he liked to throw his "back-door slider" to left-handed hitters with a full count. Gibson remembered, and that was the pitch he was looking for.

Eckersley threw the slider. He placed it low, but right over the plate. Gibson took a cut and made contact.

It was a long drive to right field.

All eyes followed the path of the ball.

Right fielder Jose Canseco turned away from the plate, indicating the ball was over his head.

"High fly ball into right field!" shouted Vin Scully. "She . . . is . . . gone!"

Kirk Gibson raised his arm over his head and held it up high. The ball landed ten rows into the bleachers, and the Dodgers had won Game 1 in a come-from-behind 5–4 classic.

Kirk Gibson circled the bases like an old man, but he was gleefully pumping his fist in the air the whole time. When he finally reached home plate the Dodgers tried to pick him up on their shoulders, but he waved them away. It would have been too painful.

What Happened Afterward

The crowd was roaring for ten minutes, until Gibson emerged from the dugout for a curtain call.

"I didn't think about a home run," Gibson told reporters after the game. "I just wanted to get the ball into play because a single would have tied it. Eckersley threw me a back-door slider down that I can hit if I stay back, and I did. And as bad as I hurt, I knew I could get myself around the bases."

Dennis Eckersley had another view of the last pitch. "It was dumb. It's a pitch I'll just have to put behind me," he said. "It was the one pitch he could pull for power. He hit the dogmeat out of it."

♦ Somebody tacked up a sign over Gibson's locker that read "ROY HOBBS." NBC replayed the home run again and again, interspersed with the final scene from *The Natural.*

"It got so I began thinking I gave up a home run to Robert Redford," cracked Dennis Eckersley.

♦ The next day, Orel Hershiser pitched a three-hit shutout, and the Dodgers led the Series two games to none.

In that game, Hershiser hit a single and two doubles, making him the first World Series pitcher since 1956 to make as many hits personally as he allowed the entire opposing team.

The pitcher who did it before was Don Larsen, when he pitched a perfect, no-hit game.

♦ Jose Canseco had predicted Oakland would win the World Series in five games, but it was the *Dodgers* who won in five games.

Oakland's feared hitters simply didn't produce. After Canseco's grand slam in the second inning, he didn't get another hit for the rest of the Series. Oakland went 18 straight innings without scoring, and hit .177 overall. They hit just two homers in the five games, while the Dodgers hit five.

♦ Kirk Gibson didn't come to the plate again for the rest of the Series.

♦ In the victory celebration after the World Series, Dodgers manager Tommy Lasorda said: "What they did here in this Series, when they didn't have the talent and they were all battered and crippled, is one of the greatest accomplishments I've ever seen anywhere. People who doubt that they can make a success in life should look to this great ball club as a role model. We did the impossible, and it could happen to you."

♦ Orel Hershiser was named MVP of the Series. He told reporters: "Today I'm living out the dream of a kid who was funny-looking, wore glasses, had arms down to his knees, and ended up playing in the majors."

♦ After his spectacular season, Hershiser had arm problems and the next four years his record was 15–15, 1–1, 7–2, and 10–15.

♦ The next season Kirk Gibson's injuries kept him down to a .213 average with just nine home runs.

♦ Dave Stewart won 20 games again the next year (21–9), making him the only pitcher to have three straight 20-victory seasons in the 1980s. Stewart made it four in a row when he went 22–11 in 1990.

♦ The A's returned to the World Series the next season. This time they *won* it, defeating San Francisco four games to one. They won the pennant again in 1990 and lost the World Series to the Cincinnati Reds. They topped their division in 1992. Dennis Eckersley saved 51 games.

♦ In 1992 the Dodgers finished dead last, for the first time since 1905.

For Baseball Trivia Lovers . . .

♦ In his World Series at bat *before* this one, Kirk Gibson *also* hit a home run. That was in the final game of the 1984

World Series, when he slammed two homers to help the Detroit Tigers beat the San Diego Padres.

♦ Before Gibson's shot, there had been seven other ninth-inning game-winning home runs in the World Series, but those had come in tie games. Gibson's was the first one that turned a loss into a win.

♦ Oakland shortstop Walt Weiss was the American League Rookie of the Year in 1988. It was the third season in a row that an Oakland player won the award. Mark McGwire won in 1987 and Jose Canseco in 1986.

♦ During the Series, TV viewers saw Hershiser in the dug-out between innings, singing hymns to stay relaxed. After the Dodgers won, Hershiser appeared on *The Tonight Show* and was coaxed into singing one.

♦ It has been said that lousy players make great managers. That proved to be true in this World Series. In his 26-game career as a pitcher, Tommy Lasorda won no games and lost four. In 1955 he tied a major-league record by making three wild pitches in one inning. Tony LaRussa had a lifetime average of .199 with no home runs in 132 games.

♦ What a season this was for Orel Hershiser! In an era when the complete game was a dying art, he threw six consecutive shutouts. His 59 straight scoreless innings broke the record set by another Dodgers great, Don Drysdale.

Hershiser also threw shutouts in the playoffs and the World Series, winning the Most Valuable Player award in each one. Naturally, he won the Cy Young award too.

♦ This was the second World Series played by two

California-based teams, and both of them involved the Dodgers and A's. In 1974, Oakland beat Los Angeles four games to one.

♦ The 1988 Los Angeles Dodgers were almost totally different from the 1987 Dodgers. These players were new to the team in 1988: Tim Belcher, Mickey Hatcher, Kirk Gibson, Mike Davis, John Tudor, John Shelby, Alfredo Griffin, Jay Howell, Jesse Orosco, Ricky Horton, Rick Dempsey, and Danny Heep.

♦ Oakland designated hitter Don Baylor didn't get into this game. But Baylor, who had waited sixteen years to play in a World Series, was participating in his third straight Series with *three different teams.*

He was on the Boston Red Sox in 1986, Minnesota Twins in 1987, and Oakland A's in 1988. All three won pennants.

♦ Hall of Famers who played in this game: As this book goes to press, none. But Canseco, McGwire, Parker, Stewart, Eckersley, and Gibson have a shot after they retire from baseball.

♦ When he was healthy, Kirk Gibson could *run*. He won a game against Montreal that August when he scored from second base on a wild pitch in the ninth inning.

♦ Two players in this game hit home runs in their first major-league at bat—Oakland catcher Terry Steinbach and Dodgers outfielder Mike Marshall. On Marshall's shot, the umpires ruled it a double. Later, outfielder Jack Clark, who was closest to the play, admitted the ball had bounced out of the stands.

Want to Read More About These Stories?

About the Shot Heard 'Round the World:

The Home Run Heard 'Round the World by Ray Robinson (HarperCollins, 1991).

The Giants Win the Pennant! The Giants Win the Pennant! by Bobby Thomson (Zebra Books, 1991).

The Great Chase: The Dodgers-Giants Pennant Race of 1951 by Harvey Rosenfeld (McFarland & Company, 1992).

Nice Guys Finish Last by Leo Durocher (Simon & Schuster, 1975).

Bums: An Oral History of the Brooklyn Dodgers by Peter Golenbock (Putnam, 1984).

The Giants of the Polo Grounds by Noel Hynd (Doubleday, 1988).

About the Fisk Game:

Beyond the Sixth Game by Peter Gammons (Houghton Mifflin, 1985).

Fenway by Peter Golenbock (Putnam, 1992).

About the Haddix Game:

The Milwaukee Braves: A Baseball Eulogy by Bob Buege (Douglas American Sports Publications, 1988).

The Great No-Hitters by Glenn Dickey (Chilton, 1976).

About the Mazeroski Game:

The Mick by Mickey Mantle (Doubleday, 1985).

About the $15,000 "Slide":

Glory Fades Away: The Nineteenth Century World Series Rediscovered by Jerry Lansche (Taylor Publishing, 1991).

Nineteenth Century Stars (Society for American Baseball Research, 1989).

Primitive Baseball by Harvey Frommer (Atheneum, 1988).

A. G. Spalding and the Rise of Baseball by Peter Levine (Oxford University Press, 1985).

About the Houston Marathon:

The Greatest Game Ever Played by Jerry Izenberg (Holt, 1987).

About the Alexander Game:

Ask your librarian for the October 9, 1978, issue of *Sports Illustrated*. It contains an interview Donald Honig did with Cardinals third baseman Les Bell, who reminisces about the World Series 52 years earlier.

About the Mazeroski, Haddix, and Hartnett games:

The Pittsburgh Pirates by Bob Smizik (Walker & Company, 1990).

About the Gibson Game:

Out of the Blue by Orel Hershiser (Wolgemuth & Hyatt, 1989).

There is an excellent video, *The History of Baseball*, which depicts some of these games. It was produced by Major League Baseball Productions. Ask about it in your local video store.

Also, it's fun to look up these games in the newspaper from the day after they took place. Ask in the microfilm department of your library to see if they are available.

Index

PLAYERS AND OTHER PEOPLE

Aaron, Henry, 1, 24, 32, 51, 55, 58, 61, 62, 64, 67, 134
Adcock, Joe, 51, 52, 56, 58, 61–62, 63, 64
Aguilera, Rick, 118, 119, 120, 133
Alexander, Charles (writer), ix
Alexander, Grover Cleveland, 1, 158–82
Ames, Leon, 66
Anderson, Dave, 195–96
Anderson, Larry, 124
Anderson, Sparky (manager), 31, 32, 35, 40, 47
Angell, Roger (writer), 36
Anson, Adrian "Cap," 1, 100, 104, 106–7, 110, 112
Armbrister, Ed, 32
Armstrong, Neil, 4
Ashburn, Richie, 56
Ashby, Alan, 118

Backman, Wally, 123, 125, 127, 128, 132
Bankhead, Tallulah (actress), 8
Barker, Len, 65–66
Barr, George (umpire), 153
Bass, Kevin, 118, 123, 130–32
Baylor, Don, 203
Belcher, Tim, 188, 189, 190–91, 192, 203
Bell, Lester, 164, 165, 167, 168, 173
Bench, Johnny, 30, 33, 34, 36, 38, 41, 47
Bennett, Charlie, 111
Berra, Yogi, 1, 13, 74, 76, 77, 80, 82, 85, 89
Billingham, Jack, 32
Blanchard, Johnny, 73, 77, 85
Borbon, Pedro, 35
Bottomley, Jim, 163–64, 165, 181
Boyer, Clete, 77, 89–90
Boyer, Cloyd, 90
Boyer, Ken, 90
Bradley, Hugh, 47

Branca, Ralph, 1, 15, 17–21, 22, 23
Brecheen, Harry, 50
Brocklander, Fred (umpire), 122
Brown, Mace, 149, 150, 151–54
Browning, Tom, 66
Bryant, Clay, 140, 141, 142
Buckner, Bill, 43, 114
Bunning, Jim, 65
Burdette, Lew, 51–59, 64, 65, 66
Burgess, Smoky, 56, 58, 72, 80
Burleson, Rick, 35, 43
Burns, Tommy, 101, 104
Bushong, Doc, 105, 107

Calhoun, Jeff, 127–28
Campanella, Roy, 11, 24
Canseco, Jose, 1, 187, 188, 189, 191–92, 194, 199, 200, 202, 203
Carbo, Bernie, 35, 36
Carroll, Clay, 34
Carter, Gary, 1, 117, 118, 120, 121–22, 123, 125, 129, 130, 131, 133, 134
Caruthers, Bob, 99–106
Castro, Fidel (Cuban leader), 30
Cavarretta, Phil, 150
Chalmers, George, 160, 182
Christopher, Joe, 62
Cimoli, Gino, 77–78, 79
Clark, Jack, 203
Clarkson, John, 100–107, 111, 112
Clemente, Roberto, 1, 52, 72, 79, 80
Cleveland, Grover (president), 180
Coates, Jim, 79, 80
Cobb, Ty, 146
Collins, James "Ripper," ("Rip"), 140, 141, 142, 143, 147
Combs, Earle, 90, 162–63, 164, 166, 167, 173, 181
Comiskey, Charlie, 104–5, 110, 112
Corrigan, Red, 148
Costas, Bob (sportscaster), 186
Covington, Wes, 52, 58
Cox, Billy, 12, 16

Crandall, Del, 51, 52, 58
Cronin, Joe, 155
Crosby, Bing (singer), 91
Cruz, Jose, 118

Dalrymple, Abner, 105
Darcy, Pat, 40, 41
Dark, Alvin, 14, 15, 16
Dascoli, Frank (umpire), 63
Davis, Glenn, 118, 129, 130
Davis, Mike, 195–98, 203
Dean, Dizzy, 139, 143, 152
Delahanty, Ed, 10
DeMaestri, Joe, 79, 81
Demaree, Frank, 149
Dempsey, Rick, 203
DiMaggio, Joe, 46
Ditmar, Art, 88
Doran, Bill, 117, 120, 126, 128, 129,
    130
Doyle, Denny, 37, 38
Drago, Dick, 39
Dressen, Charlie, 16–17, 18
Drysdale, Don, 202
Dugan, Joe, 166
Durocher, Leo (manager), 1, 5, 12, 13,
    15, 16, 18, 21
Dykstra, Lenny, 1, 120, 128, 133

Eastwick, Rawly, 35, 36, 37
Eckersley, Dennis, 1, 187, 194–99,
    200, 201, 203
Ehmke, Howard, 66
Elster, Kevin, 129–30
Erskine, Carl, 15, 17
Essegian, Chuck, 36
Evans, Darrell, 134
Evans, Dwight, 35, 39–40

Face, Elroy, 54, 75–76, 77, 78, 84
Fisk, Carlton, 1, 26–47, 76
Ford, Whitey, 74, 88
Foster, George, 34, 37, 38
Foutz, Dave, 101, 102–3, 104,
    107
Foxx, Jimmy, 155
Fregosi, Jim, 133
French, Larry, 145
Friend, Bob, 81

Frisch, Frank, 160
Furillo, Carl, 12

Garner, Phil, 117–18
Gehrig, Lou, 1, 10, 90, 155, 161, 165,
    167, 168, 179, 181, 182
Geronimo, Cesar, 34
Gibson, Debbie (singer), 188
Gibson, Kirk, 1, 184–203
Giles, Warren, 64, 65
Gooden, Dwight, 118
Gore, George, 99, 101–2
Griffey, Ken, 30, 33, 34, 39, 40, 47
Griffey, Ken, Jr., 47, 90
Griffin, Alfredo, 203
Groat, Dick, 72, 74, 76, 79, 80, 83
Groza, Lou, 91

Hack, Stan, 142, 144, 148
Haddix, Harvey, 1, 48–67, 81, 89
Hafey, Chick, 164, 165, 166, 181
Haines, Jesse, 162, 163, 165, 166, 167,
    168, 169, 181
Hamilton, Jeff, 195
Handley, Lee "Jeep," 141, 146
Haney, Fred (manager), 56, 62
Harris, Slim, 66
Hartnett, Gabby, 1, 139–55
Hartung, Clint, 16, 20
Harvey, Doug (umpire), 116, 189–90
Hatcher, Billy, 117, 118, 120, 126,
    127, 128–29, 132
Hatcher, Mickey, 190, 203
Havlicek, John (basketball player), 91
Heep, Danny, 123, 203
Henderson, Dave, 188, 191
Herman, Billy, 143, 148, 155
Hernandez, Keith, 1, 121, 123, 129,
    133, 134
Hershiser, Orel, 186, 188, 189, 193,
    197, 200, 201, 202
Hinkle, Clarke (football player), 91
Hoak, Don, 51, 52, 57, 59, 60, 64, 73,
    74, 90–91
Hobbs, Roy (fictional player), 197,
    200
Hodges, Gil, 10, 12, 14–15
Hodges, Russ (announcer), 20
Holmes, Thomas (reporter), 177
Holton, Brian, 193

Holtz, Lou (football coach), 91
Hoover, J. Edgar (FBI director), 8
Hornsby, Rogers, 1, 161, 162, 163, 167–71, 175, 177, 178, 181
Horton, Ricky, 203
Howard, Elston, 74
Howell, Jay, 203
Hoyt, Waite, 162, 163, 164, 165, 166, 181
Hubbard, Glenn, 191
Hubbell, Carl, 155
Huggins, Miller (manager), 166, 167, 181
Hughes, Tom, 66
Hunter, Catfish, 65

Irvin, Monte, 11, 15, 24

Jackowski, Bill (umpire), 86
Jackson, Reggie, xi
Jansen, Larry, 13, 24
Jerpe, Andy (fan), 86
Johnson, Darrell, 34
Johnson, Davey (manager), 119–20, 124, 127, 128, 132, 133, 134
Johnson, Howard, 132
Jorda, Lou (umpire), 24
Joss, Addie, 50
Jurges, Bill, 140, 142, 143, 144, 146, 147, 148

Kahn, Roger (writer), ix
Kelly, Mike "King," 1, 98, 99, 101, 104, 106–7, 111, 112
Kennedy, John F. (president), 4, 87
Kimber, Sam, 57
King, Martin Luther, Jr. (civil rights leader), 4
Klinger, Bob, 140, 141, 147
Knepper, Bob, 117, 119, 120, 121, 124, 132
Knight, Ray, 1, 122–32
Koenig, Mark, 163, 164, 167, 173, 177
Koufax, Sandy, 65, 126
Kubek, Tony, 75, 76, 77, 78–79, 87

Labine, Clem, 8
Lanier, Hal (manager), 121, 127
Lansford, Carney, 188, 191
Larsen, Don, xi, 50, 200

LaRussa, Tony (manager), 194, 198, 202
Lasorda, Tommy (manager), 187, 188, 192, 194–96, 200, 202
Latham, Arlie, 1, 101–2, 105, 111–12
Law, Vance, 91
Law, Vernon, 71, 72, 73, 74, 75, 84, 91
Lazzeri, Tony, 90, 147–48, 155, 166, 168–72, 178–79, 180, 181
Leary, Tim, 192
Lee, Bill, 146, 154
Lindstrom, Fred, 90
Lockman, Whitey, 10, 11, 15–16, 20
Logan, Johnny, 52, 53, 56
Long, Dale, 81, 90
Lopes, Davey, 128–29
Lopez, Aurelio, 125, 127, 133
Lowe, Bobby, 10
Lynn, Fred, 31, 32, 33, 34, 35, 36, 37, 46–47

Maglie, Sal, 8–10, 11, 12, 22
Mantilla, Felix, 60, 61, 62, 64
Mantle, Mickey, 1, 70, 74, 76, 77, 81, 82, 86, 88, 134
Manush, Heinie, 146–47, 155–56
Maris, Roger, 1, 70, 74, 76, 77, 81, 88
Marshall, Mike, 192, 203
Martinez, Dennis, 66
Marty, Joe, 148–49
Mathews, Eddie, 1, 51, 55, 58, 61, 67
Mathewson, Christy, 32, 160
Mattingly, Don, 90
Mays, Willie, 1, 4–6, 10, 11, 16–17, 24
Mazeroski, Bill, 1, 59, 68–91
Mazeroski, Lew, 73, 84
Mazzilli, Lee, 133
McCarver, Tim, 44
McDougald, Gil, 81, 82
McDowell, Roger, 124, 133
McEnaney, Will, 37
McGwire, Mark, 187, 189, 192, 202, 203
McIntire, Harry, 66
McNally, Dave, 44
McNamee, Graham (radio announcer), 162, 163, 174
Medwick, Joe, 145

Mejias, Roman, 52, 54
Messersmith, Andy, 44
Meusel, Bob, 90, 164, 167, 175, 177, 181
Meusel, Irish, 181
Miller, Rick, 43
Mitchell, Kevin, 121, 132, 134
Mizell, Vinegar Bend, 89
Moore, Earl, 66
Moran, Charley (umpire), 156
Moret, Roger, 35, 36
Morgan, Joe, 1, 30, 34, 39, 43, 47
Mueller, Don, 14–15, 16
Murtaugh, Danny (manager), 75, 81, 88
Musial, Stan, 47

Nelson, Rocky, 52, 56, 60, 72, 79, 82
Newcombe, Don, 9, 10, 13, 14, 17, 21, 24
Newsom, Bobo, 66
Niekro, Joe, 91
Niekro, Phil, 91
Nixon, Richard (vice president), 87
Nolan, Gary, 30–31, 32
Norman, Fred, 32

O'Dea, Ken, 142
O'Farrell, Bob, 164, 168, 175, 177
Oh, Sadaharu, 134
Ojeda, Bob, 1, 117, 118, 119, 124, 133
Okrent, Dan (writer), ix
O'Neill, James, 103–4, 106
Orosco, Jesse, 1, 125–26, 128–29, 130–31, 133, 203

Pafko, Andy, 10, 12, 20, 55, 56, 57
Page, Vance, 144, 145
Parker, Dave, 189, 192, 203
Paschal, Ben, 166, 181–82
Peña, Alejandro, 194
Pennington, Amber (fan), 117
Pennock, Herb, 161, 166, 181
Perez, Tony, 34
Petrocelli, Rico, 32, 35, 36, 38
Pfeffer, Fred, 100–101, 102–3
Poole, Mitch (batboy), 194
Prince, Bob (announcer), 53–57, 81, 83, 85, 86

Reagan, Nancy (First Lady), 188
Reagan, Ronald (actor), 179–80
Redford, Robert (actor), 197, 200
Reese, Pee Wee, 9, 12, 17, 24
Reynolds, Carl, 150
Reynolds, Craig, 128
Rice, Del, 58
Richardson, Bobby, 75, 76, 81, 89
Richmond, John Lee, 50
Rizzo, Johnny, 141, 144, 150
Robertson, Charlie, 50
Robinson, Jackie, 1, 9, 10, 12, 14, 15, 21, 24
Robinson, Yank, 102, 105, 107
Root, Charlie, 149, 155
Rose, Pete, 1, 30, 32, 39
Russell, Jack, 142
Ruth, Babe, xi, 1, 28, 30, 39, 88–89, 90, 94, 103, 126, 134, 149, 155, 161, 163, 167, 173–75, 177, 178, 181, 182
Ryan, Jimmy, 101, 106
Ryan, Nolan, 133

Santana, Rafael, 130
Sax, Steve, 189, 190, 193, 198
Schofield, Dick, 53, 55–56, 58, 59
Scioscia, Mike, 188, 192, 195
Scott, Mike, 1, 116–17, 119–20, 123, 124, 131, 132
Scully, Vin (sportscaster), 193, 196–97, 199
Severeid, Hank, 166
Shantz, Bobby, 74, 78, 79
Shelby, John, 192, 203
Shore, Ernie, 50
Simmons, Al, 155
Sinatra, Frank (singer), 8
Skinner, Bob, 52, 55, 56, 72, 79
Skowron, Moose, 74–75, 77, 79, 80, 83
Smith, Dave, 121, 122–23
Smith, Hal, 80
Smith, Red (writer), 25
Smith, Vinnie (umpire), 60
Snider, Duke, 1, 9, 12
Spahn, Warren, 5
Spalding, Albert (owner), 95, 96, 109–10
Stafford, Bill, 73, 74

Stanky, Eddie, 13, 21, 22
Steinbach, Terry, 189, 203
Steinbrenner, George (owner), 95
Stello, Dick (umpire), 42
Stengel, Casey (manager), 1, 71–72,
    73, 78, 79, 83, 87, 88, 91
Stewart, Dave, 187, 189, 190, 191,
    192, 193, 201, 203
Stottlemyre, Mel, 124
Stovey, Hank, 94
Strawberry, Darryl, 1, 122, 123, 125,
    127, 132, 133, 134
Stuart, Dick, 57
Stubbs, Franklin, 190
Suhr, Gus, 141, 145, 146, 156
Swift, Bill, 147
Sylvester, Johnny (fan), 178

Terry, Ralph, 83–84, 85, 87, 89
Thevenow, Tommy, 165, 166–67
Thomson, Bobby, 1, 2–25
Tiant, Luis, 1, 29–35, 46
Tiant, Luis, Sr., 30
Todd, Al, 140, 142, 143, 146, 149
Toney, Fred, 66
Traynor, Pie (manager), 145, 147,
    148, 155
Troll, William (fan), 176
Tudor, John, 203
Turley, Bob, 71, 72
Turner, Ted (owner), 95

Vander Meer, Johnny, xi
Vaughan, Joseph Floyd "Arky," 141,
    143, 145, 146, 150, 155
Vaughn, Jim, 66
Vincent, Fay (commissioner), 66
Virdon, Bill, 53, 56, 58, 59, 62, 72, 74,
    78, 79, 80
Voigt, David Quentin (historian), ix
Von Der Ahe, Chris (owner), 95, 96,
    109–10

Walker, Rube, 11, 12, 19
Walling, Denny, 129
Waner, Lloyd, 144, 149, 150, 155
Waner, Paul, 144, 147, 149, 150,
    155
Ward, John Montgomery, 50
Weiss, Walt, 191, 202

Welch, Curt, 1, 104–5, 106–7, 109
Westra, A. R. (fan), 154
Williams, Ted, 39
Williamson, Ned, 101, 103, 107
Wilson, Mookie, 120, 121, 128, 133,
    135
Wise, Rick, 40, 47
Witt, Mike, 66

Yastrzemski, Carl, 1, 31, 33, 37, 40,
    46, 47
Young, Cy, 50
Young, Pep, 141, 142, 144, 146

Zimmer, Don (coach), 38

TEAMS
Atlanta Braves, 134
Baltimore Orioles, 28, 134
Birmingham Black Barons, 5
Boston Beaneaters, 111, 112
Boston Braves, 66
Boston Red Sox, 26–47, 66, 132, 134,
    187, 195, 203
Brooklyn Dodgers, 2–25, 62, 91,
    134
California Angels, 133
Chicago Cubs, ix, 66, 111, 136–56,
    161, 176, 195
Chicago White Sox, 28, 110
Chicago White Stockings, 92–112
Cincinnati Reds, 26–47, 50, 66, 91,
    94, 181, 201
Cleveland Indians, 46, 73, 133,
    195
Detroit Tigers, 146, 202
Houston Astos, 114–35
Los Angeles Dodgers, 23, 29, 36, 65,
    184–203
Milwaukee Braves, 48–67
Minneapolis Millers, 5
Minnesota Twins, 203
Montreal Expos, 203
New Britain Red Sox, ix
New York Giants, 2–25, 90, 111, 155,
    177
New York Mets, 23, 43, 88, 114–35,
    186
New York Yankees, 13, 23, 68–91,
    112, 147, 154, 158–82

Oakland Athletics, 29, 184–203
Philadelphia Phillies, ix, 56, 160, 182
Pittsburgh Pirates, 48–67, 68–91, 136–56, 178
Pittsfield Cubs, ix
St. Louis Brown Stockings, 92–112
St. Louis Cardinals, 50, 56, 90, 111, 158–82
San Diego Padres, 202
San Francisco Giants, 23, 201
Washington Senators, 90, 155

BALLPARKS
Astrodome, Houston, 114–35
County Stadium, Milwaukee, 48–67
Dodger Stadium, Los Angeles, 184–203
Fenway Park, Boston, 26–47
Forbes Field, Pittsburgh, 68–91, 139, 154
Polo Grounds, New York, 2–25
Sportsman's Park, St. Louis, 92–112
Three Rivers Stadium, Pittsburgh, 90
Wrigley Field, Chicago, 136–56
Yankee Stadium, New York, 158–82